drawing the human head and portraits

Improve Your Painting and Drawing

Fountain Art Series. Fountain Press London

. M. Parramon

drawing the human head and portraits

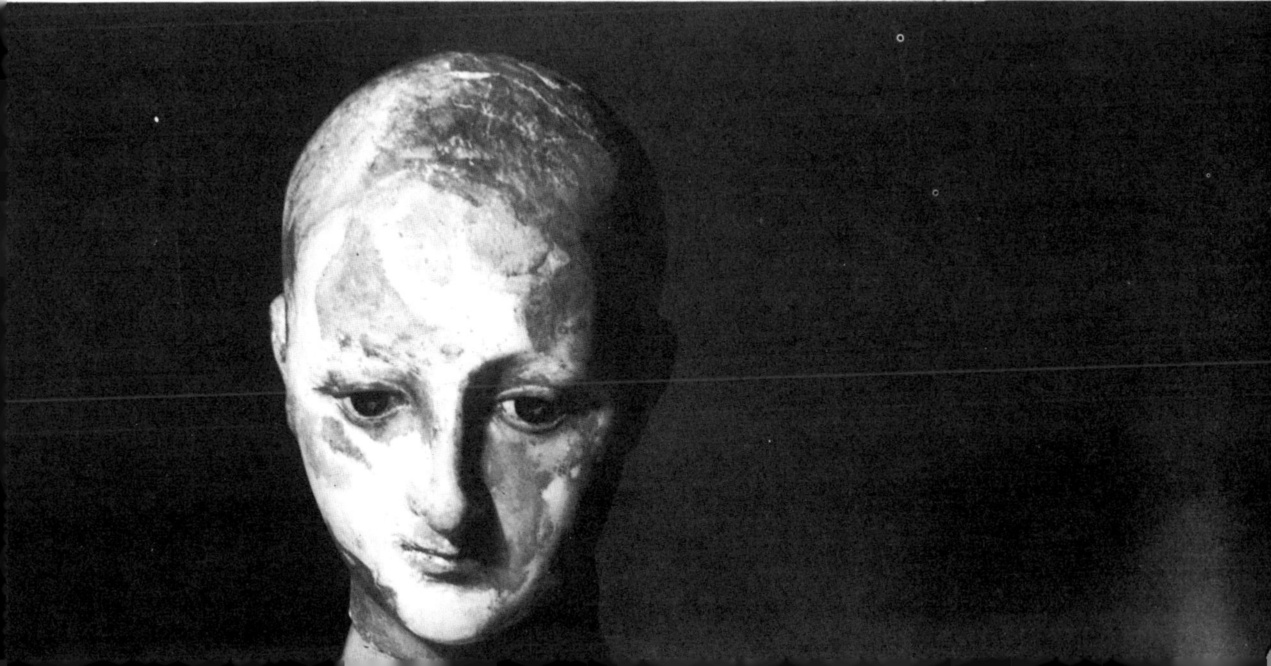

Fountain Press
Argus Books Ltd.
14 St. James' Road,
Watford,
Hertfordshire,
England

First Edition in English, 1972
Second Edition, 1979
Original title in Spanish
«Cómo dibujar la Cabeza
humana y el retrato»

ISBN O 852 42099 4

Printed in Spain by
CIAC, Mata, 32. Barcelona
Depósito Legal: B-7152-79
Número Registro Editorial: 785

CONTENTS

Bow down low before beauty.

See how man is made in God's image;

What a hard task it is to capture his

features, for God Himself decreed that

Eve should be different from Adam

and Adam different from any other man.

Yet see how easy it is, because no other

creature is so beloved, so well-remembered,

so well understood.

Ingres to his pupils.

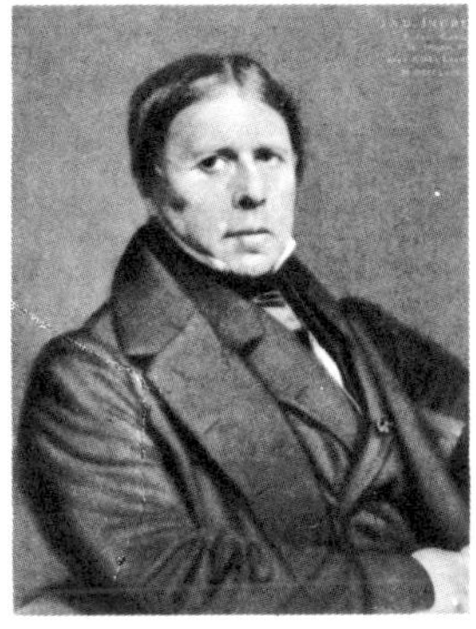

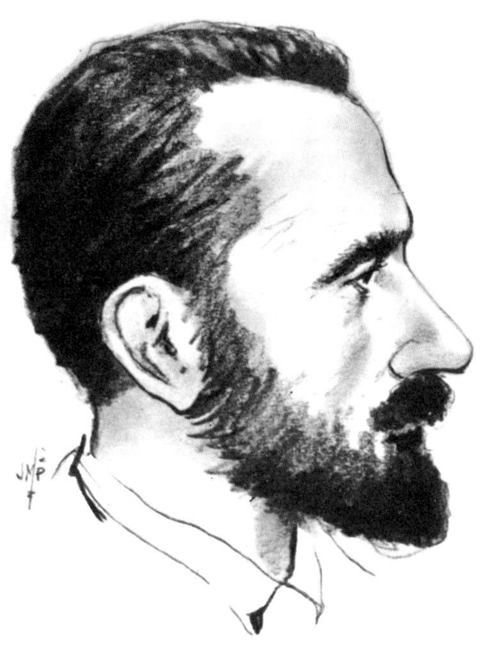

MONSIEUR BERTILLON, ANTHROPOLOGIST

Paris, a February afternoon in 1879.

At police headquarters a policeman places a pistol on the inspector's table and, pointing to a man under arrest, reports: «Marcel Dupont, armed robbery».

The inspector looks at the detainee: a well-built chap with a broad face, reddish hair, flat nose... . If this was Dupont's first offence, the sentence would be mild, otherwise his penalty would be severe. «Send him up to Monsieur Bertillon», he commands.

Monsieur Bertillon was a junior member of the staff who, three months earlier, had suggested a new identification technique based on photographs and body measurements. Now, while trying to find Dupont's face in his records, Bertillon remembers his chief's final words: «OK, try it out», he had said irritably, «but if nothing comes of it within three months, you'll have to forget the crazy notion!»

Suddenly Bertillon takes out a file, studies it and dashes to the inspector's office: «It isn't Dupont, sir! It is Martin, the escaped murderer. He has disguised his face and dyed his hair, but he wasn't able to change his bone structure».

... ...

That February afternoon saw the discovery of a new branch of anthropology, the science which studies the physical and moral nature of man. Alphonse Bertillon named it «Anthropometry».

Defining this new science, he stated: *Basically, anthropometry studies the measurements and proportions of the human body or its individual parts*. Measurements, proportions, the human frame...? How can this concern us as artists? We shall see:

ANTHROPOMETRY APPLIED TO ART

Anthropometry is in fact directly connected with the art of boxing up, constructing and drawing the human figure. In the first place, it demonstrates that every body is different. If we study the possible variations of an ear, for instance, we find twenty different types which, when combined with five types of nose and seven shades of eye-colour, etc., produce such a variety that it is impossible to find fourteen which bear any close resemblance. At this stage, we simply realize that, when drawing John, we are faced with dimensions different from those of Peter.

But luckily, anthropometry has benefited us in another way: in addition to morphology (the science of form) and anatomy, it has worked out the proportions of thousands of bodies, comparing race, sex and age; it has studied the measurements used by painters and sculptors throughout the ages; it has provided the artist of today with a better knowledge of the body's dimensions and proportions.

For example, the scientist, Von Lange, has recorded the height of a million men and found that 300,000 have an average height of 5 ft. 5 ins., 400,000 of 5 ft. 9 ins. and 300,000 are over 5 ft. 9 ins. Lange also fixed the height of the head at 8 ⅞" and ascertained that the size of the head is the most constant measurement of all parts of the body, being between 8 ¼" and 9 ½". Richer, Stratz and Fritsh, among other scientists, have carried out countless surveys, comparing present-day man with major sculptures of Greece and contemporary art and thus scientifically determining the natural and artistic canon for the human body.

This is a great help, as we shall see:

CANON FOR THE HUMAN HEAD

In order to draw the head, we must study its general measurements and proportions. To determine these, scientists and artists use what is called the «canon».

By CANON we mean the rule or system which determines and relates the proportions and dimensions of the human figure on the basis of a general unit of measurement called a MODULE.

As an example of this, look at Fig. 1. This shows the proportions of the human body following an «eight head» canon, as drawn by Albert Dürer, the 16th-century German artist. (In this case the basic module or measurement is the height of one head).

The canon, or rule of proportions, is derived from comparative studies, like those mentioned earlier. Through them it determines the ideal proportions as seen by the man in the street, or by the artist, altering them as needed to reproduce a more typical model (3).

The canon is a great help to us as regards both proportions and construction. We shall show how in the next section.

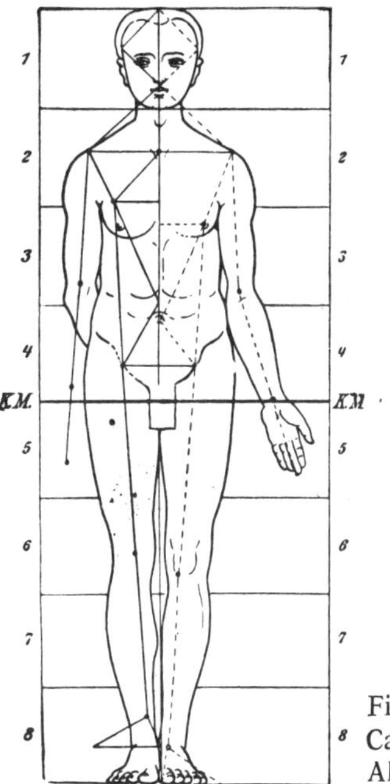

Fig. 3.
Canon.
Albert Dürer.

Ideal proportions of the human head

Let's think of a perfectly proportioned (and imaginary) head which typifies the ideal. Let's look at it full-face and in profile as it might have been in the records of the celebrated Monsieur Bertillon (Figs 4 and 5).

Right? Now let's study the canon which I used to draw it.

Please have a really good look, because the rules which follow are rather like a magic formula. Together with further suggestions and illustrations, they will enable you to draw a head as simply as a vase or a chair. It's a good plan to have a pencil and paper by you, so that you can practise and make notes.

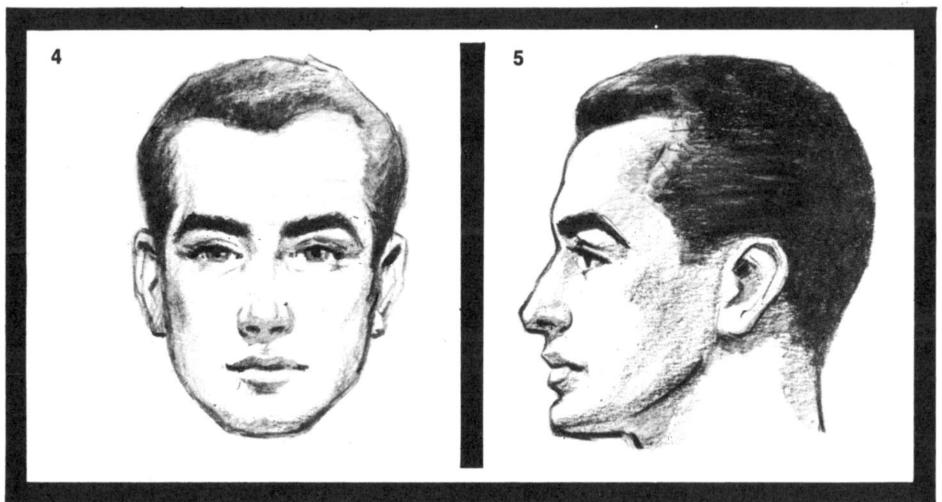

(1) We recommend *Drawing the Human Body* in this series. It contains a detailed examination of the proportions, construction and method used for drawing the human figure; it also helps you to draw the human figure from memory.

CANON OF THE HUMAN HEAD

The following canon of proportions applies to any adult head, male or female, young or old. It does not apply to the head of a child. This will be studied later.

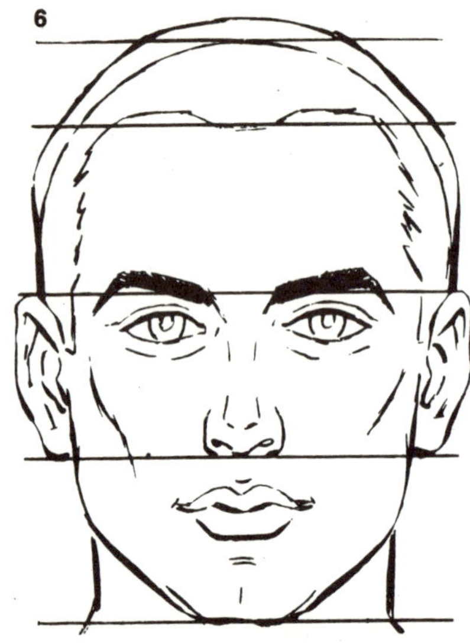

Fig. 6. — Notice first of all that the canon of this head is three and a half times the height of the head. So when you come to draw a head, you can say:

If we divide the height of the head into 3½ units and draw guidelines, we get the position and proportions of the following:

A) *The upper profile of the head or cranium, omitting the hair.*

B) *The hair-line.*

C) *The lower part of the nose.*

D) *The lower section of the face.*

E) *The positioning of the ears.*

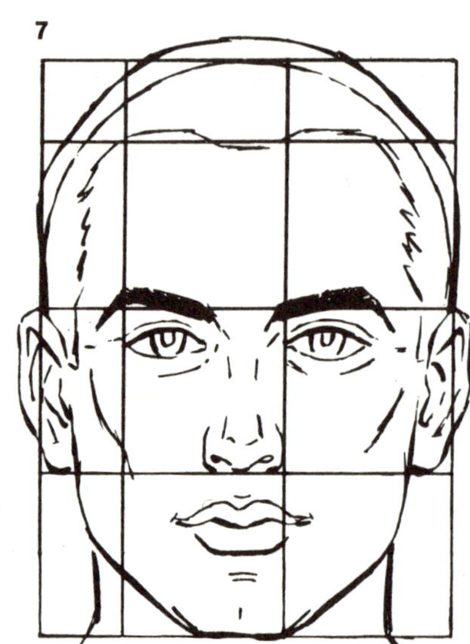

Fig. 7. — Now we can see that the forehead module divides the width of the head into 2½ units. We can thus formulate the following rule:

When viewed from the front, the height and breadth of the human head form a rectangular box measuring 3½ units high by 2½ units wide. (Example: taking 2" as the unit, we get: 2 × 3.5 = 7" high by 2 × 2.5 = 5" wide).

Why not try doing this yourself?

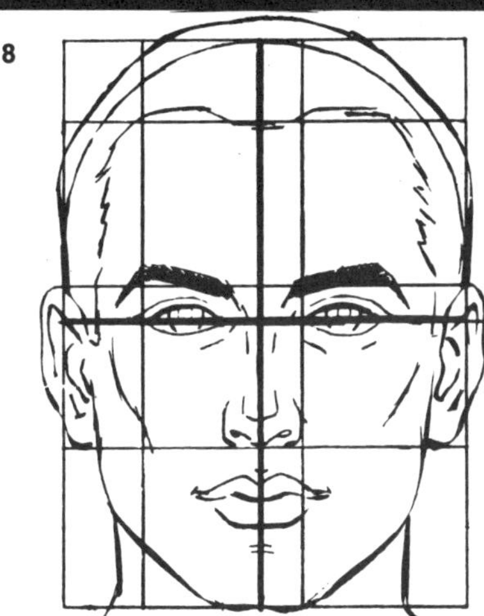

Fig. 8. — If we now fix the vertical and horizontal centre of the rectangular box, we find that the nose and mouth lie on the vertical centre line and the eyes on the horizontal line. From this we can deduce the following important rule:

The eyes are situated exactly half way up the head.

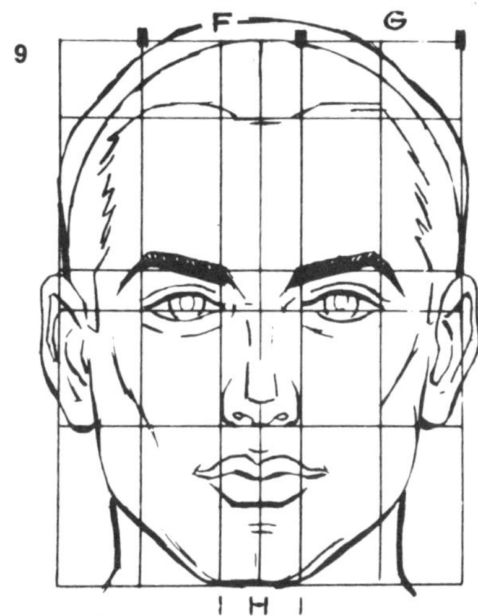

Fig. 9. — By dividing the modules F and G into two parts (i.e. by dividing the total width of the rectangle into parts) we can fix the size of the eyes. Notice —and this is extremely important— that the distance between the two eyes equals the breadth of one eye, just as if there were a third eye in the middle. The breadth of the chin (shown as H) is shown to be more or less equal to one-fifth of the total width of the head.

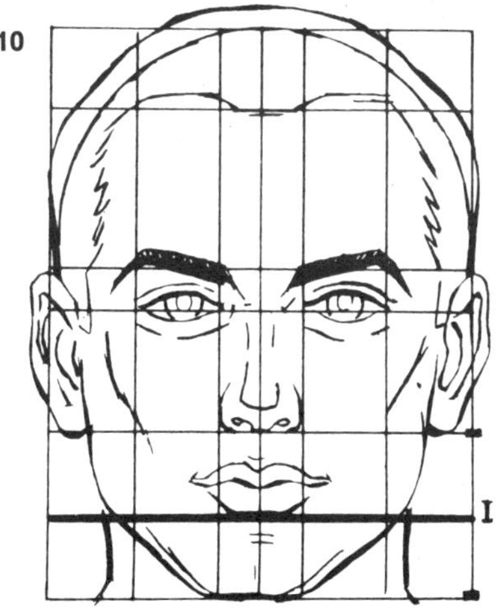

Fig.10. — Finally, the lower lip is situated on a line dividing the basic module or unit I into two equal parts. This is the last feature of the canon governing the front view of the human head. It is a very simple formula for boxing up and fixing proportions.
Now we shall deal with the same head in profile.

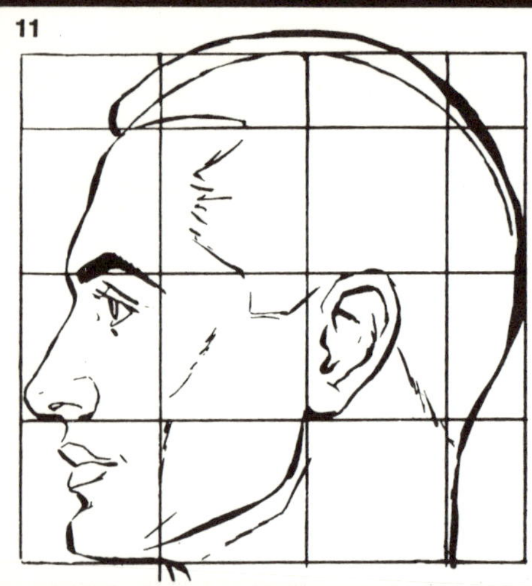

Fig. 11. — Using the same canon, we can see that the total height and width of the head equal three and a half times the height of the forehead. So:

The dimensions of a human head in profile form an exact square.

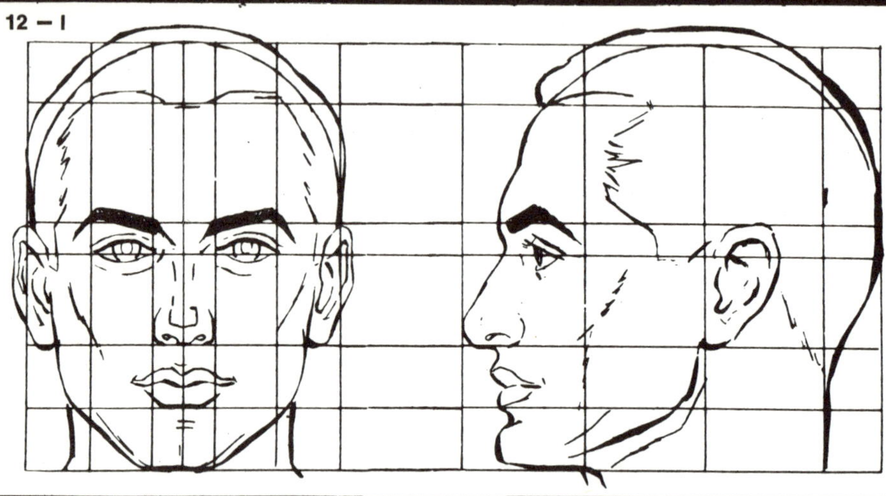

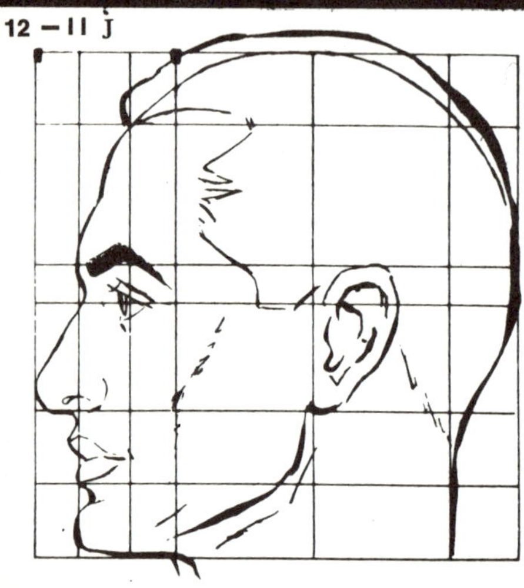

Fig. 12. — As regards the position and correct proportions of the features (eyes, nose, mouth, etc.) you need only remember:

I. — To fix the position of the eyebrow, eye, nose, ear and mouth, you can use the same horizontal lines as for the full-face view.

II. — By subdividing the module or unit into three parts we obtain various reference points which enable us to draw the facial angle and also confirm the position of the eyebrow, eye, nose, etc.

Have *you* tried drawing a head this way? It's easy, isn't it?

But don't be satisfied with drawing just one head. Do it over and over again until you can manage without referring to the illustrations. This is the first, vital step towards learning how to draw the head and face.

THE HUMAN HEAD IS SYMMETRICAL

Here is another general principle to be borne in mind.

We have, in fact, a pair of eyes, a pair of ears, cheek bones, etc., which, when seen from the front, have identical shapes and measurements and appear to be separated by single features, the nose, mouth and chin, so that if we draw a line down the centre of the front view of a face on the left we shall have a duplicate, but back to front image of that on the right.

You will say that this is a statement of the obvious, but it leads on to an extremely important conclusion:

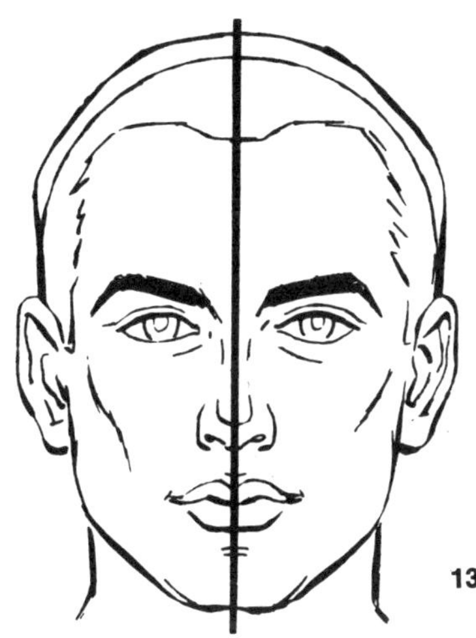
13

Because of the symmetry of the human head, a basic line of reference can always be drawn through its centre. We shall call this: THE SYMMETRICAL CENTRE OF THE FACE.

On this symmetrical centre the proportions and structure of the face are based. But first we must examine the notable shape formed by...

THE HUMAN SKULL

We shall dispense with the usual list of bones which starts with the frontal and ends with the prominent feature of the cranium, passing through the zygomatic process, because —with due respect to some books and systems which seem to have been thought up by doctors rather than artists— I would like to suggest that osteology, the science of bones, is not a subject for the draughtsman.

We must study the human skull with the sole object of drawing it and need only remember its general shape and mechanism. We must bear in mind that the human skull is shaped as in Figs. 12 and 13.

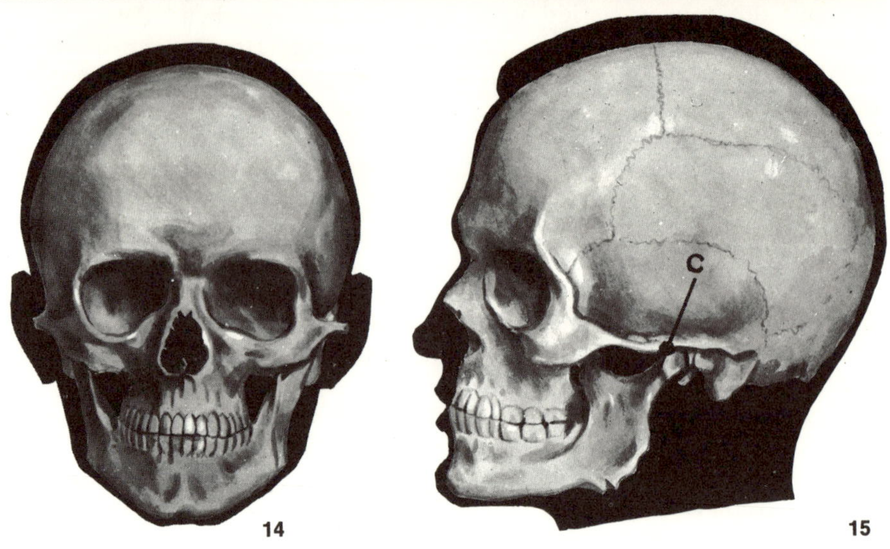

14 15

We must notice that its shape is influenced by its structure, which cannot be said of other parts of the human skeleton. If we examine the black outline round the skulls in Figs. 12 and 13 —it represents the external limits of the head— we can see that in the jawbone, cheekbones, forehead and scalp the muscles and tissue are not at all bulky, so it is the shape of the skull itself which determines the contours.

Therefore, when we draw the human head we must first think of the skull, since this is *the basic shape we must use in order to draw the head correctly.*

The illustration of the skull also reminds us that it is made up of two basic parts —the cranium and the lower maxillary (consisting of the jawbone and chin). The latter is the only movable section, the only one which moves when we open and close our mouth to speak, eat, laugh, cry, etc.

But since this is connected with expression, to be considered later, let us now return to the question of boxing up and analysing the human skull, leaving out the details and studying only the basic framework.

Basic structure of the human head

Seen in profile, the human head can be reduced to a simple sphere with the jawbone below it, with line A sloping by some 80° —representing the angle of a white man's face. Then, assessing by eye the three and a half modules (remember what you studied earlier) and marking these on the sloping line, we can immediately fix the position and proportions of the nose, mouth, eye, etc. (Fig. 17).

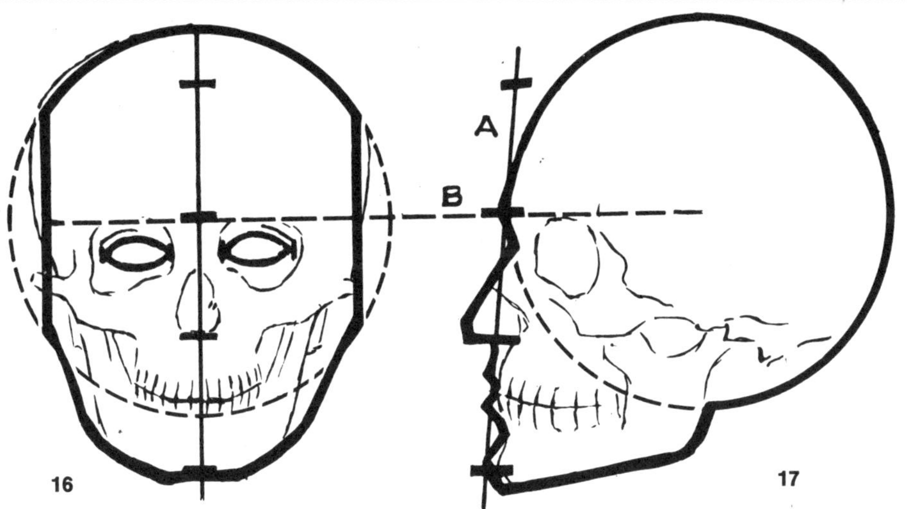

In the front view of the head the basic sphere is slightly altered and flattened at the sides. The rest of the framework is provided by the shape of the jawbone and the line we have decided to call *The symmetrical centre of the face,* along which we can work out the three and a half divisions to fix the position and proportions of the various features. Notice how, in this case, when boxing-up, we fix the position of the eyes, or rather the eye, by rough measurement —remembering that the eye is below the brow, that the width of each eye is one-fifth of the face and that the eyes are one eye's-width apart (Fig. 16).

During this boxing-up exercise you should note the placing of line B, which positions the eyebrows. In both front view and profile, this line is seen to bisect the sphere.

CONSTRUCTION OF THE HUMAN HEAD

A word of warning! There is no point in going on to this section unless you are proficient at the previous exercises. Sorry to rub this in, but I am certain that these rules will enable you to solve, once and for all, the tricky business of drawing the head and face. If we start afresh, bearing in mind what we have just studied, we can now see how to box up a head irrespective of its angle.

First of all, visualise the sphere of the skull with an axis through its centre (Line A). (In this and the following illustrations I am giving you various examples of the head at different angles. Thus the sphere

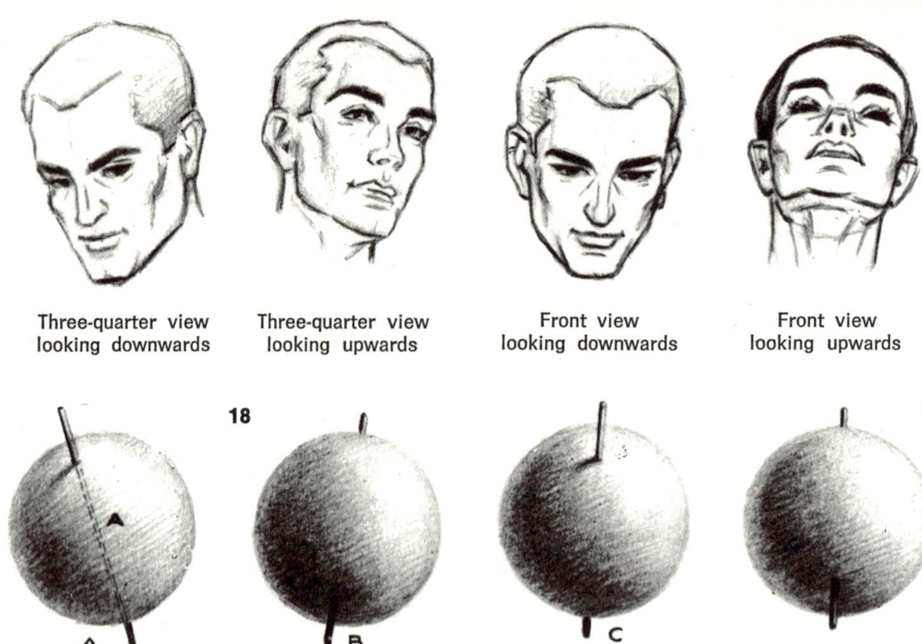

marked A corresponds to the three-quarter view of a head looking slightly downwards: B is a head looking upwards, again showing a three-quarter view, while C is looking downwards (Fig. 18).

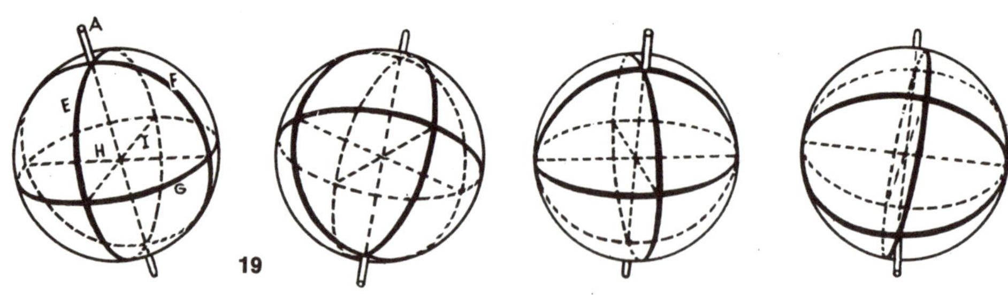

Divide the sphere by two vertical ellipses starting from the axis A (E, F); and then a horizontal ellipse (G). From this latter circle trace the two crossed lines (H, I) at a right angle from the axis A, keeping the correct perspective. To make things simpler, we are thinking of the sphere as transparent. It is important to practise drawing spheres in perspective freehand by eye, not with a ruler and set square (Fig. 19).

(2) We recommend *Drawing in perspective* in this series, which gives a simple and readable explanation of all the other rules concerning perspective.

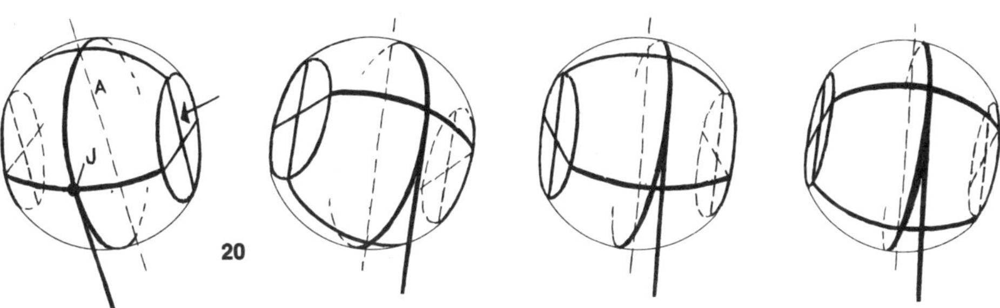

Now imagine that you slice off a little bit from each side of the sphere to produce a rather flattened shape. On these flat sections draw straight lines which continue the course of the circles (shown by an arrow). At the same time mark the «symmetrical centre of the face» from point J, extending it downwards in parallel with the axis A (Fig. 20). Now we have to divide the «symmetrical centre of the face» into three and a half units or modules. Study carefully how these divisions are made, allowing for foreshortening, i.e. the fact that we are looking at a face which is tilted downwards, upwards, sideways, etc.

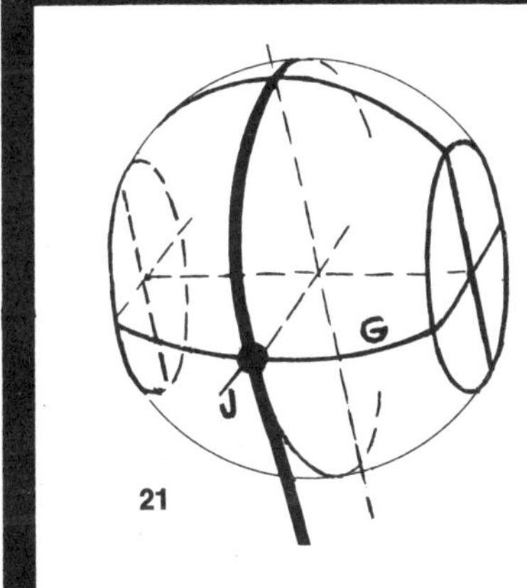

First of all notice that the point J, at which the line marking the symmetrical centre begins, also lies on the circle G. See how this circle forms the centre —that is the centre in perspective— of the sphere and remember that, as we have seen in Figs. 16 and 17, this circle or dividing line determines the exact position of the eyebrows (Fig. 21).

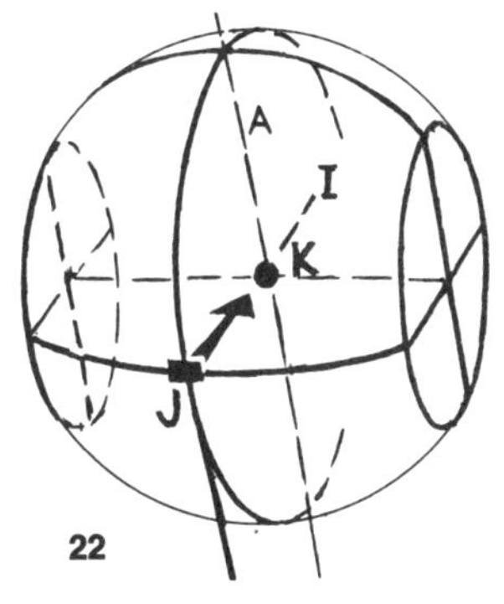

Notice too that, owing to the slope of the line I, we find no difficulty in joining point J to the geometrical centre of the sphere, K. Finally, note that this point K lies naturally along axis A which runs through the sphere and shows us its position (Fig. 22).

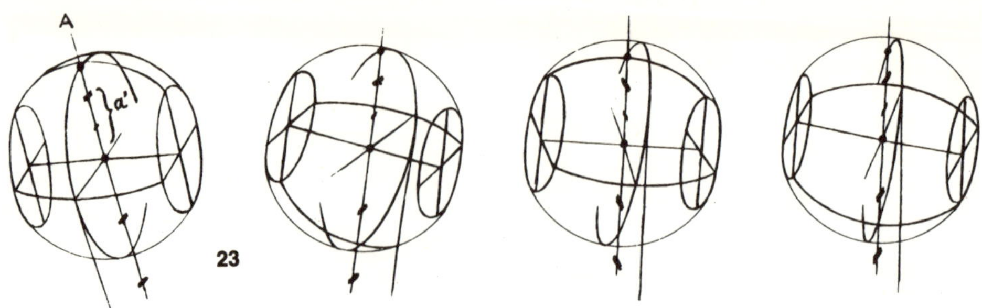

Start by calculating the three and a half divisions along axis A as if the axis were the symmetrical centre of the face. To do this, first divide the upper half into one and a half units —or modules— and from the centre downwards mark off two sections equal to the module in (Fig. 23).

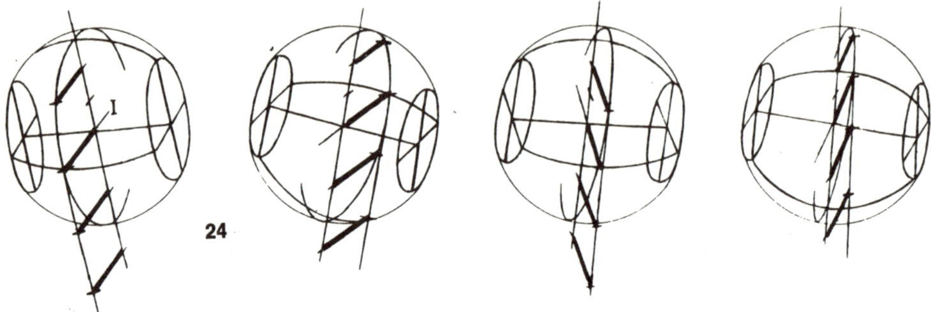

When you have marked these divisions, transfer the points to the line corresponding to the symmetrical centre but —and this is the key to the problem— keep the angle of perspective shown by the line I, that is to say, draw the other lines parallel to line I (Fig. 24).

It's easy —we have now marked along the symmetrical centre of the face the canon of proportions for foreshortened views, irrespective of the angle of the face.

(You may be wondering whether a professional artist really has to do all this in order to draw a head. In a way he does: if the artist is drawing or painting from life, he may not need these formulae, but, if he is drawing from memory, they may be necessary and, if the angle of the head produces a very foreshortened view, they would be more or less essential. I say «more or less» because it always depends upon the artist's talent and experience. But the competent professional will know these rules and apply them, possibly in his mind's eye, instead of in black and white).

Where were we? Oh, yes... .

Now we have to draw the jawbone. We must take a little time in order to capture its special shape, which depends upon the position and foreshortening of the face. We shall first examine the basic form of the jawbone or, to use a better term, the movable bone known as the lower maxillary. To go back to our skull:

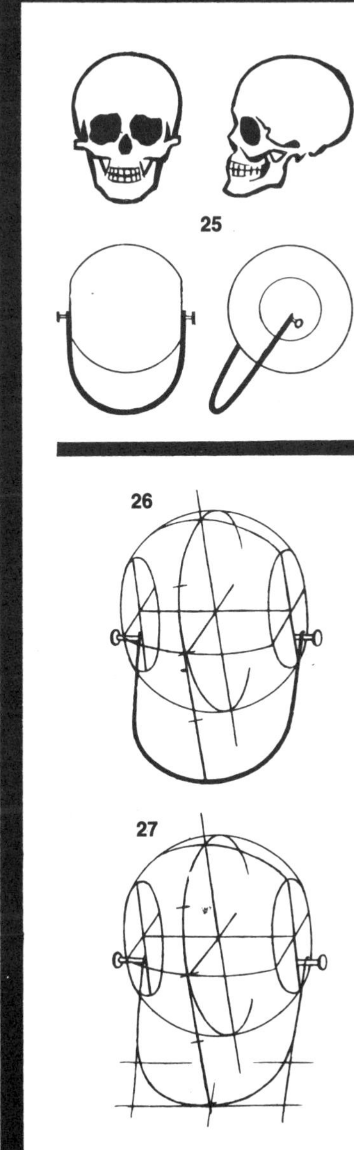

For simplicity, we could consider the lower maxillary as a horseshoe (Fig. 25).

Is it difficult to visualise this horseshoe as if it were the lower maxillary, hanging from the sphere? Imagine a nail protruding from each ear and then imagine that those nails are holding a horseshoe, which swings so that its lowest part touches the chin... and there you are (Fig. 26).

An easier method is to draw the semicircle of the horseshoe within a rectangular box which is formed in perspective and then, inside the rectangle, mark the curve of the horseshoe, also in perspective. It's simplicity itself. Anyone can draw the sloping horseshoe irrespective of the angle of the face. The only point you have to watch is that the outermost part of the arc always coincides with the theoretical position of the chin, which, in turn, is shown by the lowest division along the symmetrical centre of the face (Fig. 27).

Having solved this first problem, let's look at the way this horseshoe can be elaborated to resemble the lower maxillary.

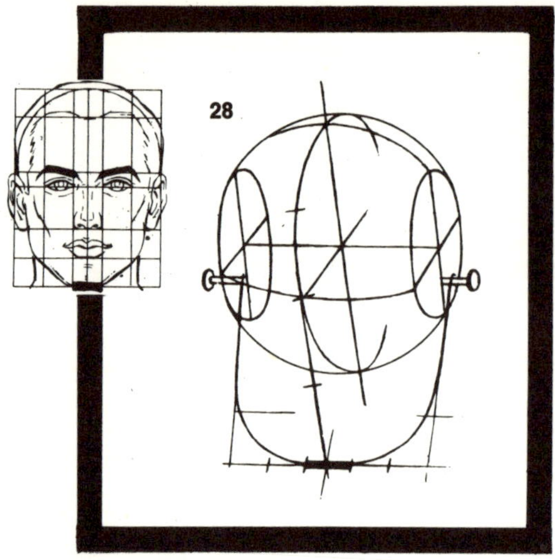

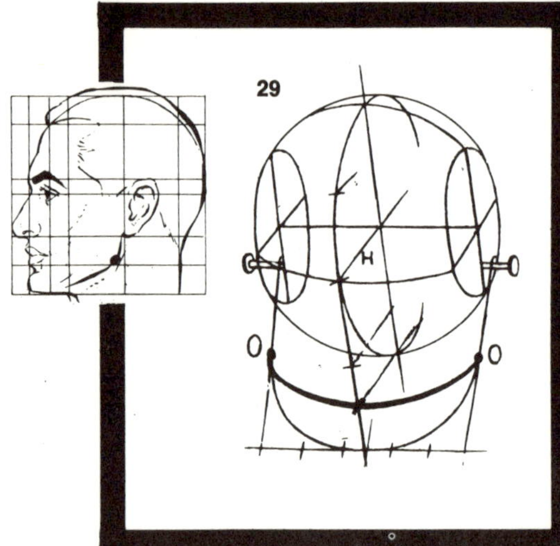

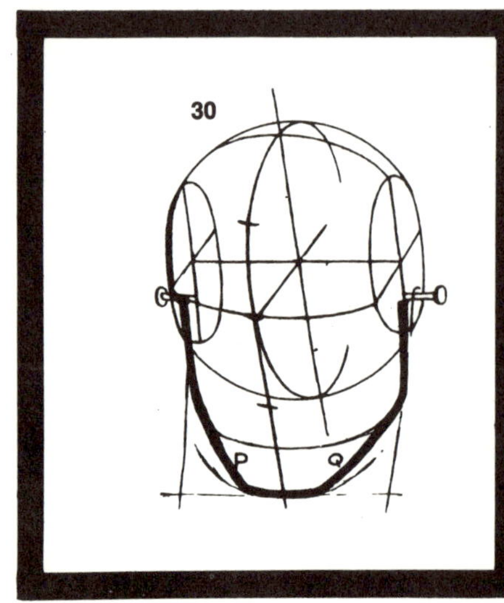

Do you remember how, in the canon we studied earlier, the width of the chin was equal to a fifth of the face? So, by dividing the width of the lower part of the horseshoe into five parts, and using the middle of these five parts, we should locate the lower line and width of the chin (Fig. 28).

We can see that the most prominent and angular section of the lower maxillary (O) lies more or less level with the mouth... slightly below it, if we want to be precise. By chance we have a perfect line of reference for this position, namely the middle of the lower module of the face. So we need only extend that line of reference to the central axis A, keeping the correct perspective, parallel to the cross-line H, and we have these two most prominent points of the lower maxillary (Fig. 29).

The rest is easy: on one side draw the two sloping lines P and Q which mark the lower edge of the jawbone and, on the other side, drop two short straight lines from the ear openings, remembering that these lines must be parallel to the axis A (Fig. 30).

So there is no difficulty in forming the lower maxillary and all that's left is a few small —but essential— touches to improve and adjust its general shape. Notice the position, form and size of the cheekbones in relation to the outer form of the jawbone. Pay special attention to this feature, which always —or nearly always— plays a part in the character of the face you are drawing.

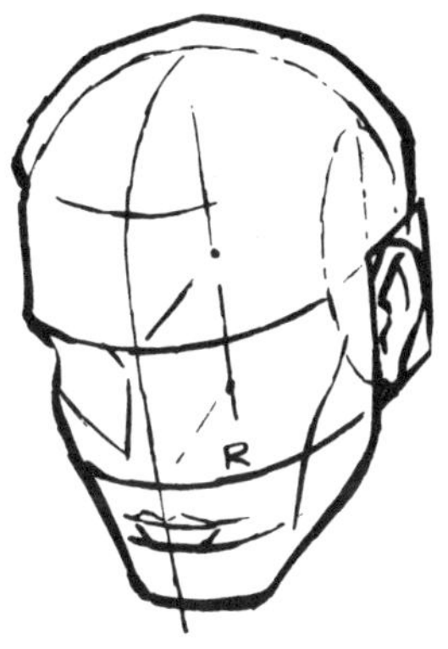

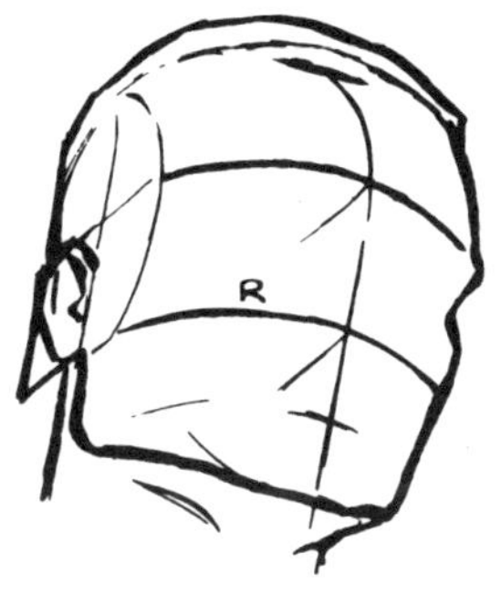

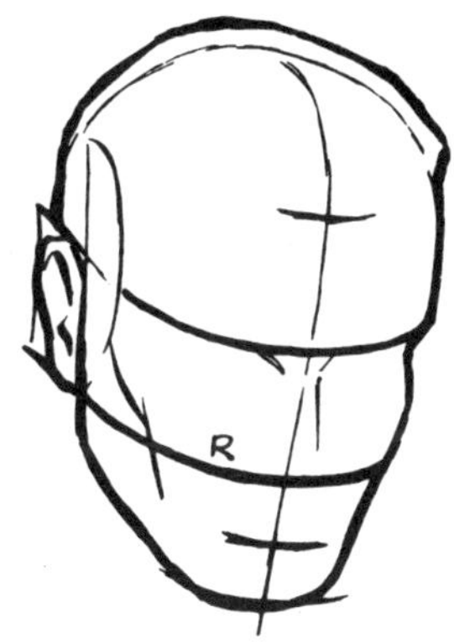

31

To continue with the boxing up, draw the circle R in perspective, following the curve of the jawbone parallel to the circle above it. As you will recall, the position of these two circles fixes the position of the eyebrows and the length of the nose and, at the same time, provides the height and position of the ears. In Fig. 31 notice how the ear is framed by a rectangle in perspective whose vertical lines are parallel to the axis A. In the centre of the lower module draw the small curve for the position of the mouth. Remember that this curve is simply the line mentioned in Fig. 10 when we were studying the canon. It gives us the outline of the lower lip (Fig. 31).

Now we already have the basic structure, having placed the dividing lines of the canon in perspective, so we can draw on these lines the various features in their proper proportions: eyebrows, eyes, nose, mouth... the ears have already been positioned correctly.

The eyebrows do not call for much comment. They are placed along the central circle of the sphere. They present no problem and you will see them in all the drawings used to illustrate the following pages.

The eyes, however, are much more tricky:

We know that they lie exactly halfway up the head, but now we have to see how they are positioned in relation to the ears and nose when the head is looking downwards or upwards; we must consider the effect caused by foreshortening, which places the eyes on a different plane from the eyebrows... but we shall deal with this in stages:

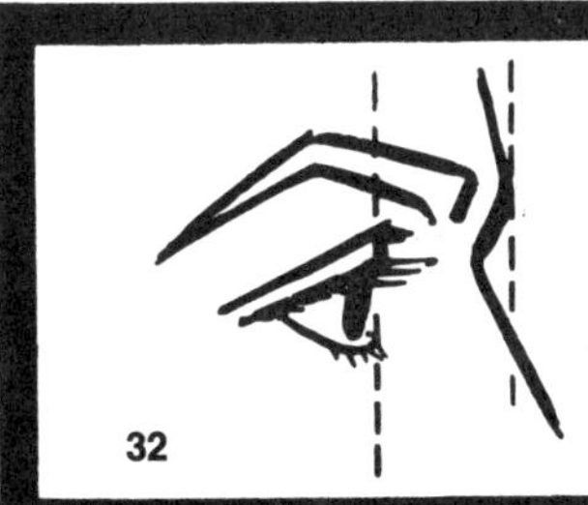

32

First of all see how the orbits of the eyes, and thus the eyes themselves, lie on a plane behind the forehead and eyebrows. This drawing shows what I mean.

Bear in mind that, when the head is bent forward, the hollow containing the eyes makes them look as if they were underneath the brows, almost hidden. Sometimes we can't even see the upper plane of the orbit, i.e. the distance between the eyebrows and the eyelids (Fig. 34 on the opposite page).

On the other hand, when the head is bent back, we look almost straight at the plane of the orbits, so that the eyes appear to be at a greater distance below the eyebrows (Fig. 35 on the facing page). You'll notice in Figs. 34 and 35 the same sort of changes in the shape of the nose, mouth, cheekbones, cheeks, etc. Their size varies considerably as the head is tilted further forward or backward.

We can now go on to the shape of the nose, which is comparatively easy to sketch in, as we can see from the following illustration:

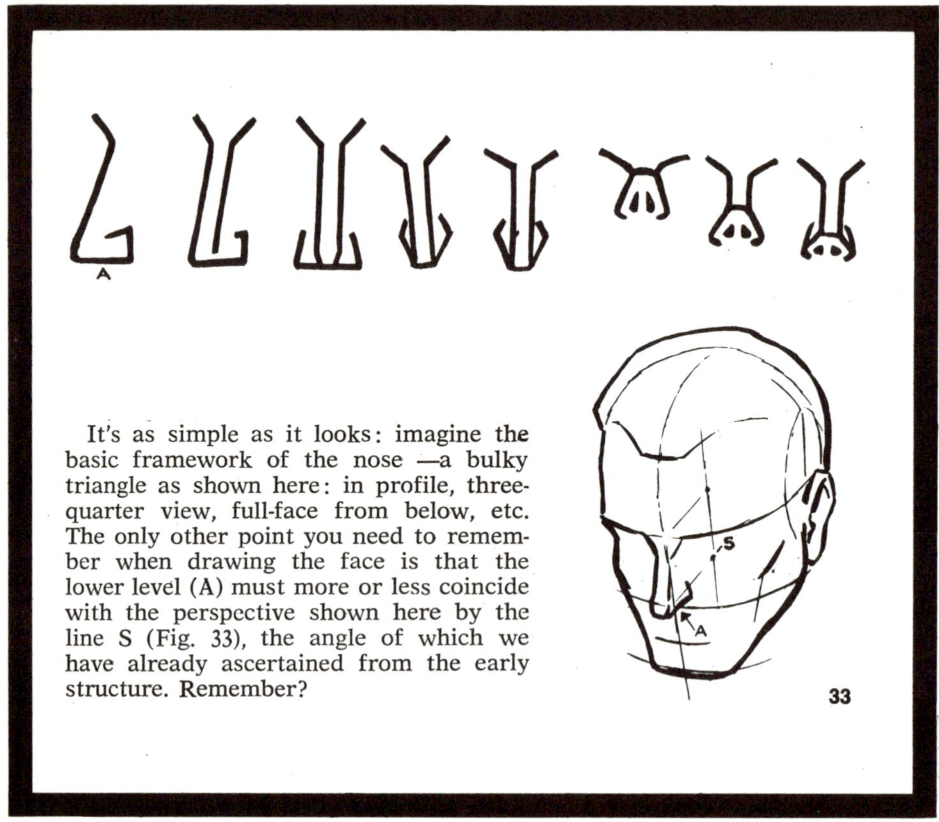

It's as simple as it looks: imagine the basic framework of the nose —a bulky triangle as shown here: in profile, three-quarter view, full-face from below, etc. The only other point you need to remember when drawing the face is that the lower level (A) must more or less coincide with the perspective shown here by the line S (Fig. 33), the angle of which we have already ascertained from the early structure. Remember?

Finally, the shape of the mouth; the hairline, its shape at the temples, the sideboards, etc. Examine these shapes in the drawings in Fig. 36 where we show the final versions of different heads and different positions and summarise everything you have learnt about this fascinating process.

This completes our study of the human head as far as boxing up is concerned. Of course, we have not gone into details or examined individual characteristics. The next section will deal with these, but before we go on, I would like to give a final piece of advice on the construction of the human head:

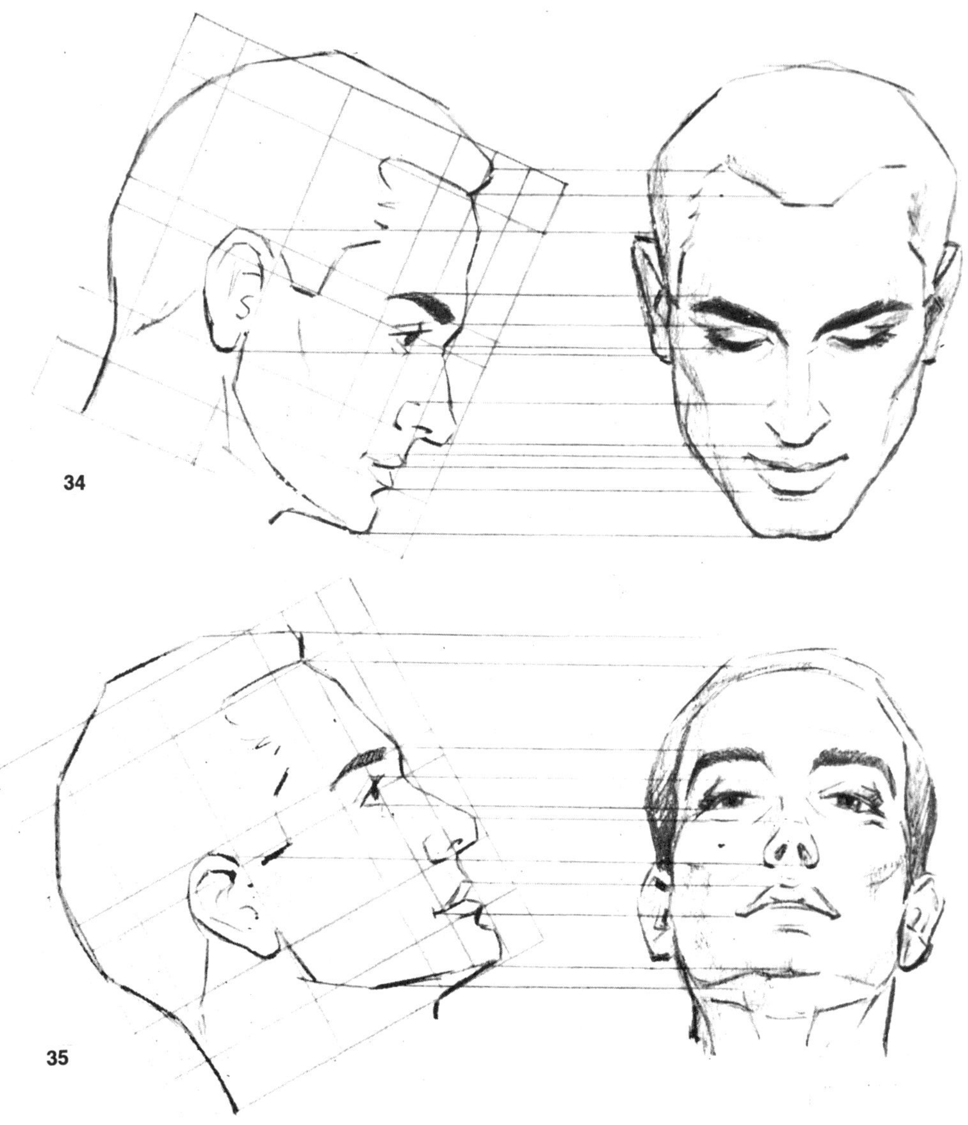

ALWAYS TRY TO VISUALISE THE OTHER EAR

When you draw a head in profile, half-profile, three-quarter view, etc., positions in which you can see only one ear, always think of the other, invisible ear. That other ear should act as a symbol for all the parts of the face hidden from view. «To think of the other ear» is the same as drawing both ears, both eyes, both sideboards, the entire lower maxillary... just as if you were drawing a transparent head. Think of them as being on the same plane as the ear, eye, sideboard, etc. on the side you are actually drawing.

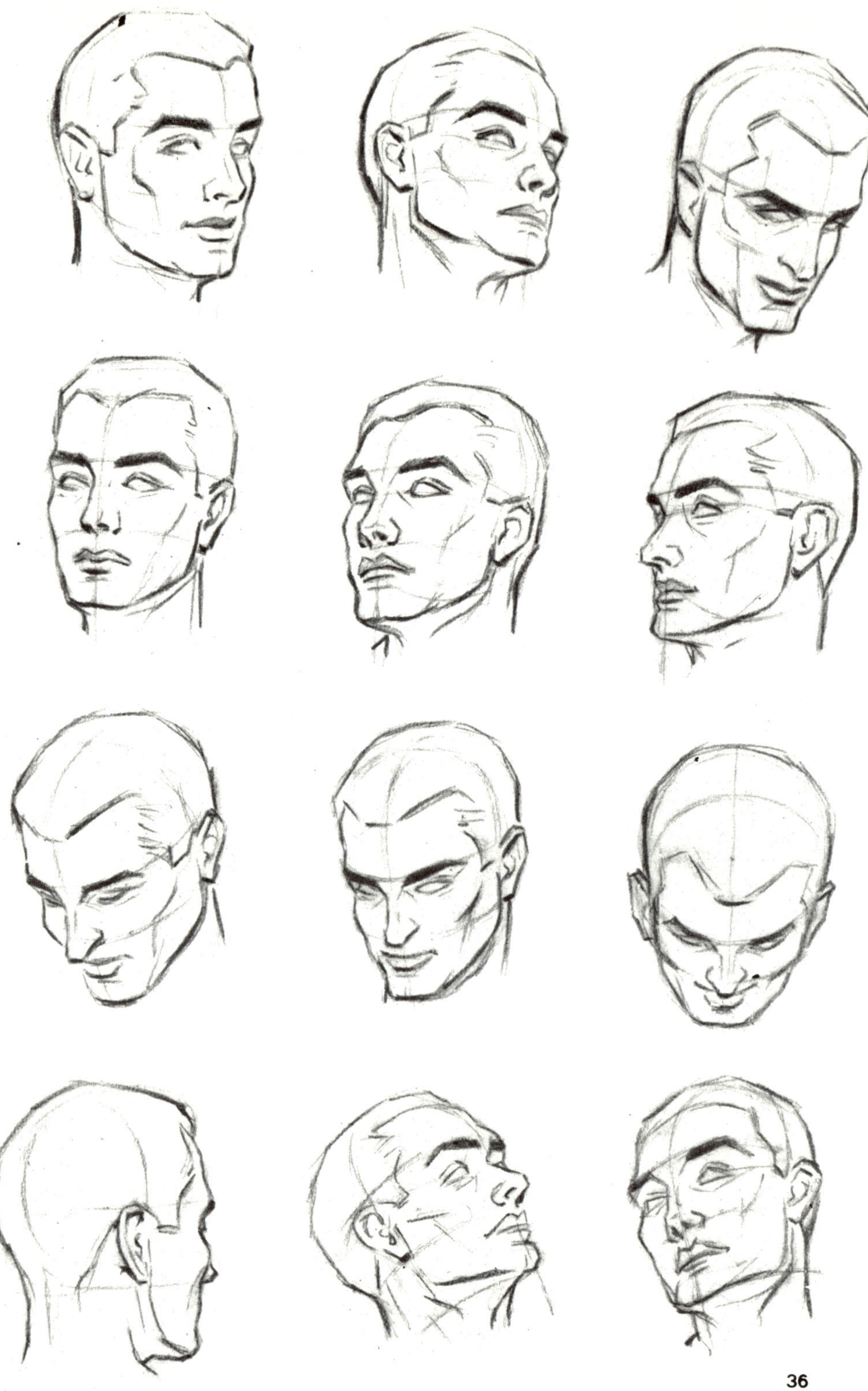

36

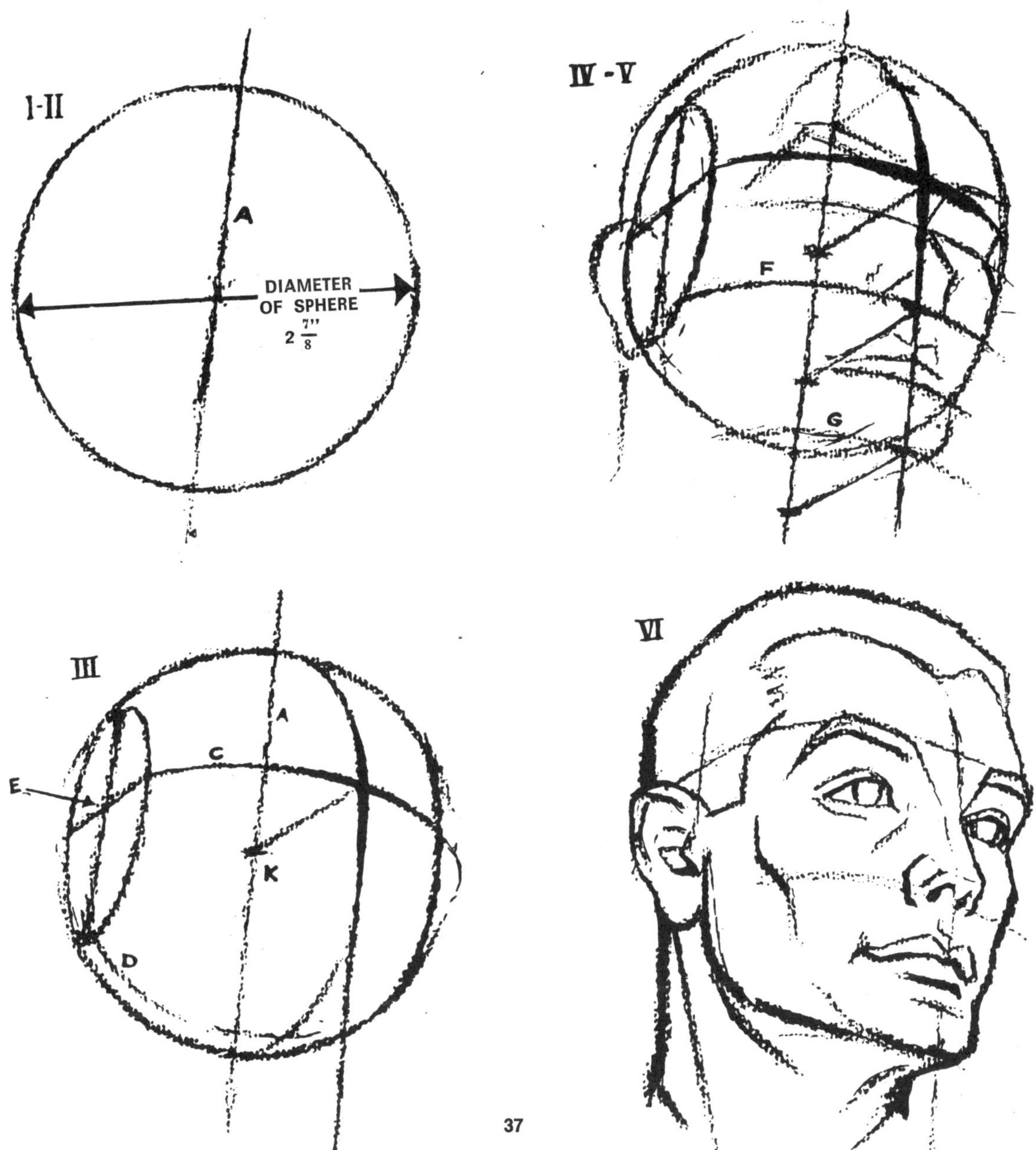

To summarize: try to draw a head by following these instructions:

I and II: Draw the sphere by freehand: fix the angle of the axis A. Fix the position of the space between the eyebrows in order to get the position of the circles B and C.

III: Cut a slice off both sides of the sphere; fix the position of point K in the centre of the sphere: extend the line forming the symmetrical centre.

IV: Divide the axis A into three and a half units starting from K and transfer those divisions onto the symmetrical centre of the face. Work this out by eye. Then draw the curves for the position of the nose and ear (F); and, finally, the lower line of the chin (G).

V: Rub out the preliminary lines which are not needed for the rest of the structure. Visualise the lines of the canon which determine the proportions of the head when seen from the front.

VI: Finally draw in the features, remembering the general instructions given in the previous pages.

AGE AND SEX OF THE HUMAN HEAD

AGE, GROWTH AND PROPORTIONS OF THE HUMAN HEAD

We start by asking ourselves why, when compared with an adult, a new-born child has a large head, a proportionally bigger skull, large eyes, which are wider apart, and a comparatively small nose, mouth and chin. The answer is easy: the vital parts of a new-born child, the brain, eyes, ears, etc., must fulfil their adult functions from birth. Take sight for instance: at the age of two a child should see as clearly and perfectly as you and I. So the eyes of a two-year-old must be already fully developed. The same applies to some of the internal organs, the brain and auditory system, for example. But the young child cannot chew as strongly as an adult. Why is a baby fed on cereals, soups, etc? Because it does not have the powerful masticatory muscles and strong teeth which an adult uses to chew and break hard foodstuffs. Consequently, a child's jaw is not developed *—does not need* to be developed— and is small and embryonic, just like its mouth and nose.

Let's go on to examine the changes produced in the shape of the face as a result of this clever physiological arrangement.

TWO YEARS OLD...

This is the age when differences in proportions between the child and the adult are at their greatest.

1. A child's head is large

In proportions the head of a child is larger than that of a man: if you place a twenty-five year-old man beside a two-year-old child you will see that the *actual size* of the man's head is almost twice that of the child's, while the *proportionate size,* i.e. in relation to the two bodies, of the child's head is almost twice as great as the man's.

2. A child has a very large cranium

...quite disproportionate when compared with the size of its face. We have already explained why: at this age it needs a brain to control its senses, its sight, its hearing, its touch... apart from being able to recite multiplication tables and write appealingly to rich aunts, it can do almost as much as you or I.

3. A child's eyes are large

There's no need now to explain why. But let's take a moment to study certain characteristics. Look at the shape and size of the child's eyes: they are not as slit-like as ours — when open, the eyelids almost form a circle, so that one can hardly see the pink point of the tear gland.

Remember that:

The reason why a child's eyes are so large is the size of the iris and pupil

...the ocular globe, in fact. This is because the child has a fully developed *sight organ* formed by the iris and the pupil and *not by the space below the eyelids,* which are less fully developed. These have to make a special effort by opening more widely.

For the same reasons we can see that:

A child's eyes seem to be set further apart than an adult's

Do you remember the rule that «the eyes are separated by an eye's breadth»? (Fig. 7). In a child's face this distance is greater. Don't forget this basic rule.

4. The nose is small and up-turned

A child has small lungs, narrower respiratory channels and a small nose with small nostrils. But why is it up-turned? Because the nasal bones are not as fully developed as an adult's.

5. The maxillaries are not developed

The lower maxillary, which is the primary factor determining the height of the beard area and chin, is only a small bone in comparison with an adult's powerful jawbone.

A child's teeth are smaller. This further reduces the distance between the lower section of the nose and the lower edge of the jawbone. For the same reason a child's face is made all the larger and the entire profile of the jawbone is curved.

Bearing all this in mind, you may wonder how to fix the level of the eyes. In the centre of the head like a man's? Below the centre? Above the centre? The answer is easy and very important when you get down to work:

A CHILD'S EYES ARE SITUATED BELOW THE EXACT CENTRE OF THE HEIGHT OF ITS HEAD

So, if we draw a sphere with the sides sliced off and place two large far-apart eyes below the centre of a small round face... we have a child's head. (See Fig. 40, which gives several sketches of a child's head and illustrates the points I have made.)

All we need now is to determine the position of each feature and then note the changes which take place as the child grows.

CANON FOR THE HUMAN HEAD AT DIFFERENT AGES

Two years old

We draw this head by using a canon different from the one used for a man. As you can see, the general outline of the head when viewed full-face forms a rectangle measuring three units wide by four units high. The basic unit or module is the distance between the lower part of the nose and the lower line of the chin. The eyes can be positioned by a secondary line (A) cutting the unit containing them into two equal parts.

In profile, the child's head produces a square box.

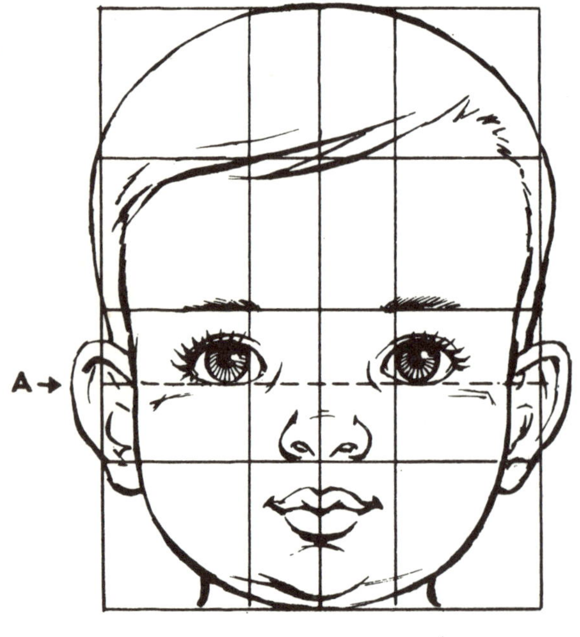

38

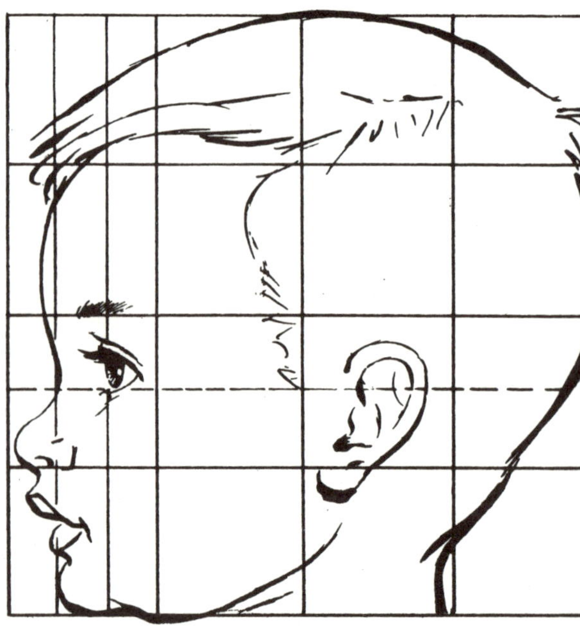

39

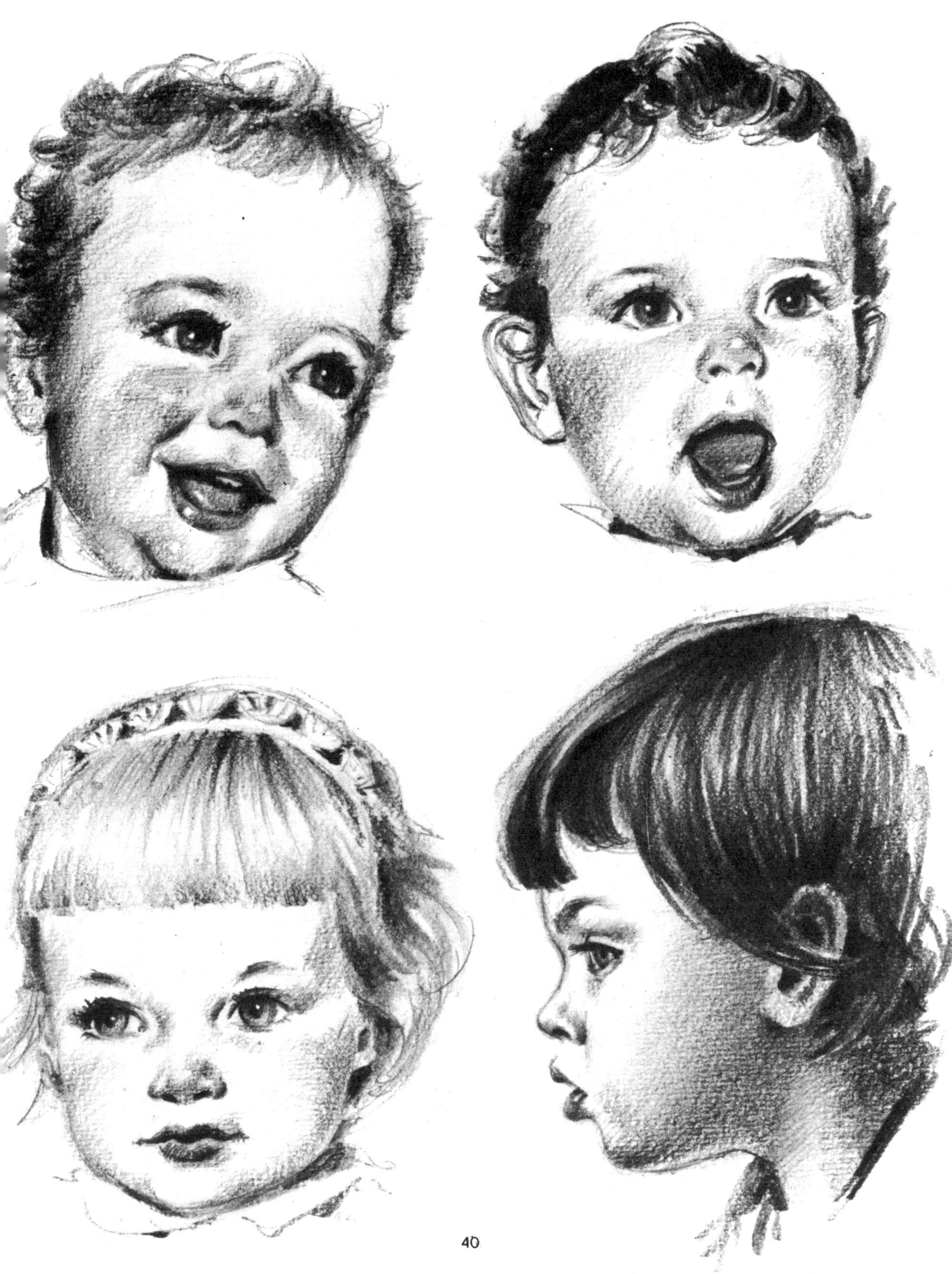

40

Growth of the human head

2 years 41

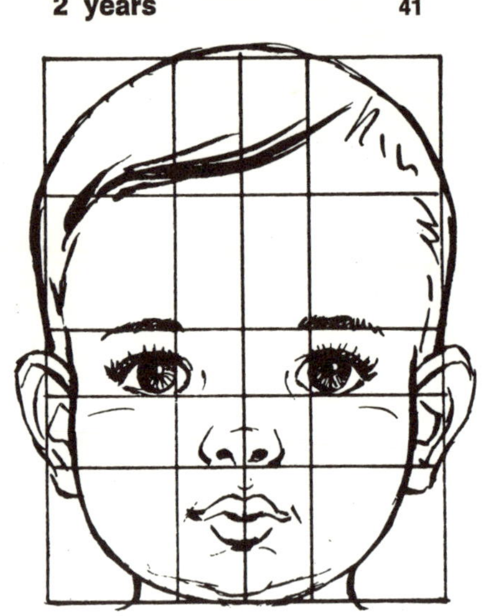

6 years 42

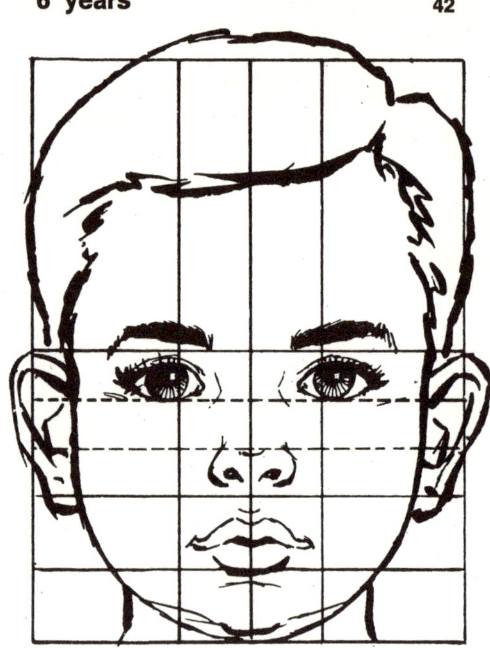

Study this head of a two-year-old child and notice the characteristics which differ from those of an adult:

a) *The high, clear forehead with the hairline well back on the top and sides.*
b) *The eyebrows,* not the eyes, *are halfway up the head.*
c) *The eyes are separated by a distance which is more than the width of one eye.*
d) *The ears are proportionally larger and are placed lower.*
e) *The nostrils are more evident.*
f) *The jawline is round, with a slight curve in the centre.*

Six years old

We can still use the previous canon, but its measurements for positioning the features are less exact. To some extent they must be positioned by eye, bearing the original rule in mind, but allowance should be made for the following changes caused by growth of the head:

a) *There is much more hair which encroaches on the forehead and temples.*

b) *The jawbone is more developed, so the face is longer than before.*

For the same reason...

c) *The eyes and eyebrows (the latter are thicker) have moved upwards.*

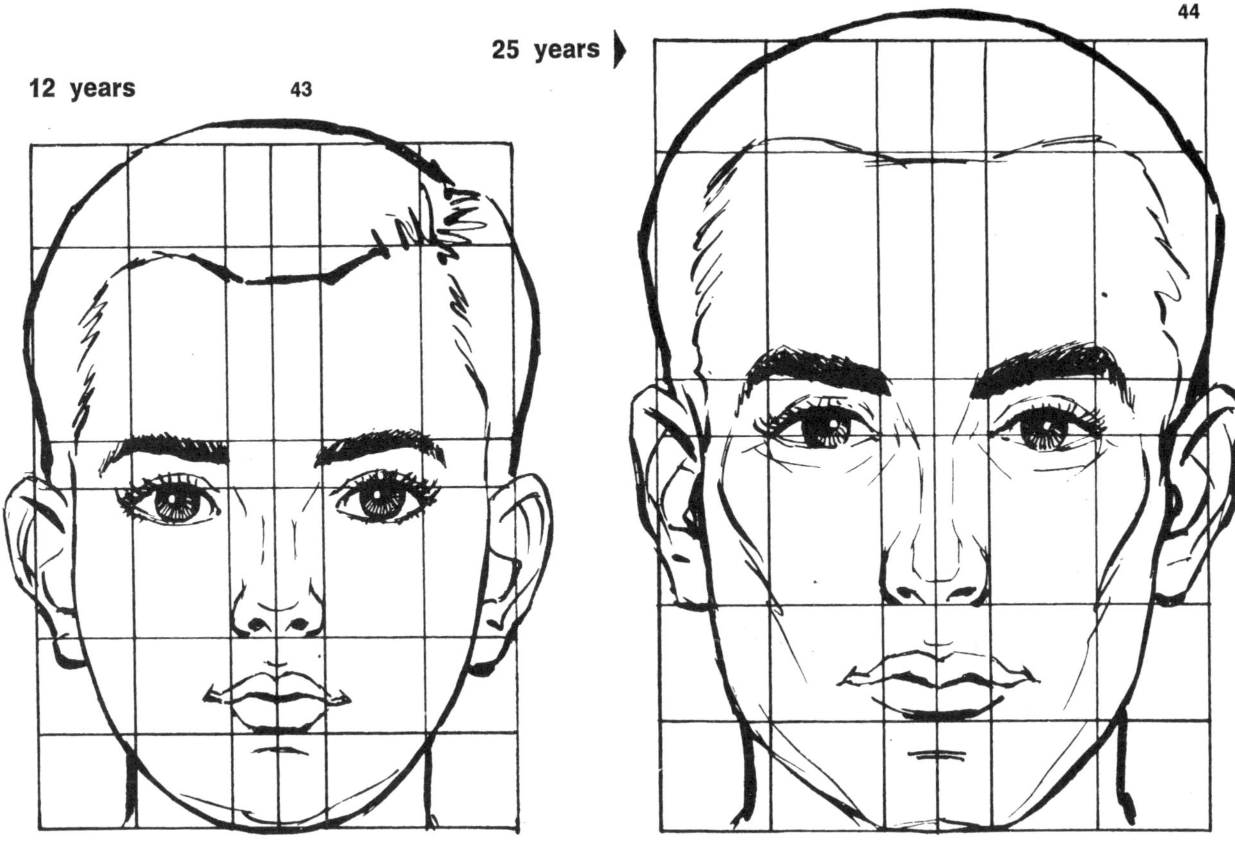

d) *The nose, mouth and ears are higher.*
e) *The jawbone still retains its curved shape.*

Twelve years old

The head is becoming more adult in shape and can be drawn using the adult canon, but less precisely.

a) *The hair is still as abundant as before, but its encroachment on the temples, an adult characteristic, is not pronounced.*
b) *The eyes and eyebrows are not yet halfway up.*
c) *Although lower than an adult's, the ears have now fully developed. They will not grow any larger.*
d) *The bone structure of the lower maxillary is becoming apparent. The jawbone is less rounded.*

Twenty-five years old

No comments are needed when you remember the canon. Just examine the structure of the face compared with the previous drawings; the eyes are more oblique and closer together (notice how the width between the eyes in Fig. 43 resembles Figs. 41 and 42 rather than the adult [Fig. 44]). The nose, cheekbones and jawbone are more clearly defined and form a more angular whole than in the child. The two could never be confused, could they?

...And at eighty

At this advanced age the fat tends to disappear and the skin contracts so that —without going into detail— the shape of the face is determined entirely by the bone structure. This produces the following general appearance:

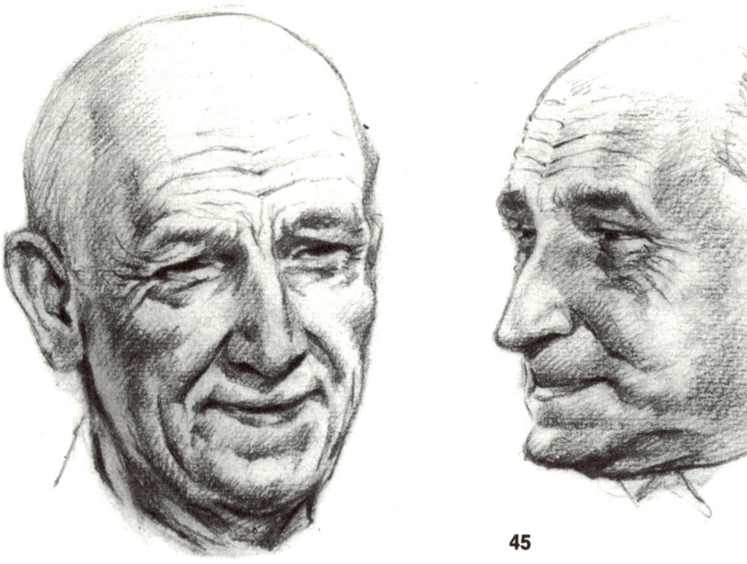

45

a) *A tendency towards baldness: clear bony forehead.*

b) *The bone structure of the temples becomes more pronounced, showing the artery.*

c) *The ocular globe and the eye in general are more sunken, making the bones over the cavities more evident.*

d) *Pouches and wrinkles around the eyes.*

e) *The cheekbones are more pronounced as the cheeks sag or become hollowed.*

f) *The nasal bones are more evident.*

g) *The lips are thinner.*

h) *Pouches and loose skin below the chin and on the neck.*

There is another important factor which can cause considerable changes in the distance between moustache level and chin, so that the former draws inwards and slightly upwards like a nutcracker. This is the lack of teeth. If the person is wearing false teeth, the facial structure is not all that different from that of a younger person. Yet, whether there are teeth or not, an older person's jaw is always inclined to be more pronounced, making the chin higher, simply because of the many thousand times the maxillaries have been pressed together.

AND, FINALLY, THE HEAD OF A WOMAN

Whatever branch of art you are planning to take up, it is probable that you will draw and paint many more women's heads than men's. You may wonder why we have left this subject until last, devoting so little space to it. But there is a good reason for doing things this way round:

The proportions of the female head are fundamentally the same as those of a male.

If we look at both types of head in their natural state —forgetting about cosmetics— we shall find very little difference between them.

Differences there are, however, and we must take them into account. They stem mainly from the physical make-up of the woman, particularly the larger amount of subcutaneous fat in the breasts, buttocks, hips and thighs and also, to a lesser extent, in the face; these are a secondary result of the fact that men lead more active lives —exercises, games, work— which is bound to produce a stronger, more virile bone and muscle structure. This is why, for instance, a man's nose is usually wider and fatter; he runs more, jumps more, etc., thus breathing more heavily, which tends to enlarge the respiratory organs, the thorax, etc.

To pinpoint these slight differences, we can say of a woman's head that:

1. **THE FACE IS SLIGHTLY SMALLER**
2. **THE EYES ARE SOMEWHAT LARGER**
3. **THE EYEBROWS ARE SLIGHTLY HIGHER AND ARCHED**
4. **THE NOSE AND MOUTH ARE SMALLER**
5. **THE JAW IS ROUNDED**

Getting down to brass tacks, we can make the following generalisation to emphasise the vital difference between the male and the female head.

This is a rule which the artist should always bear in mind:

A WOMAN'S HEAD AND FACE ARE COMPOSED OF SOFT LINES AND CURVED FORMS

Angularity is a sign of masculinity, while curves, smoothness and fluid shapes are basically associated with femininity.

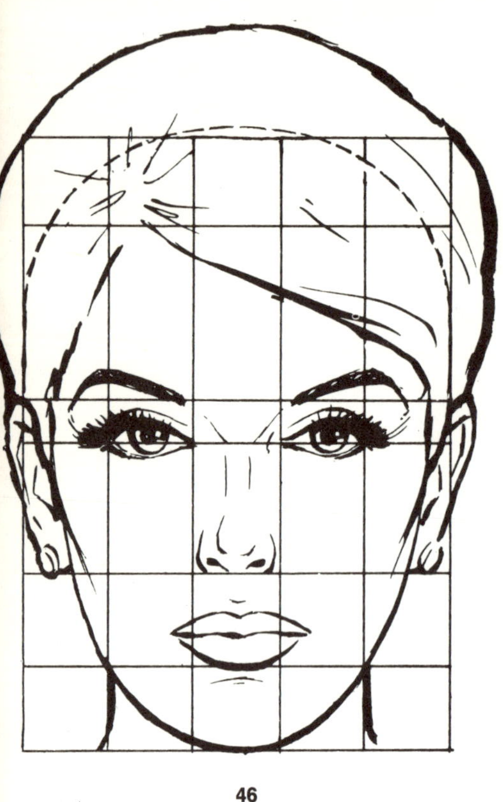

46

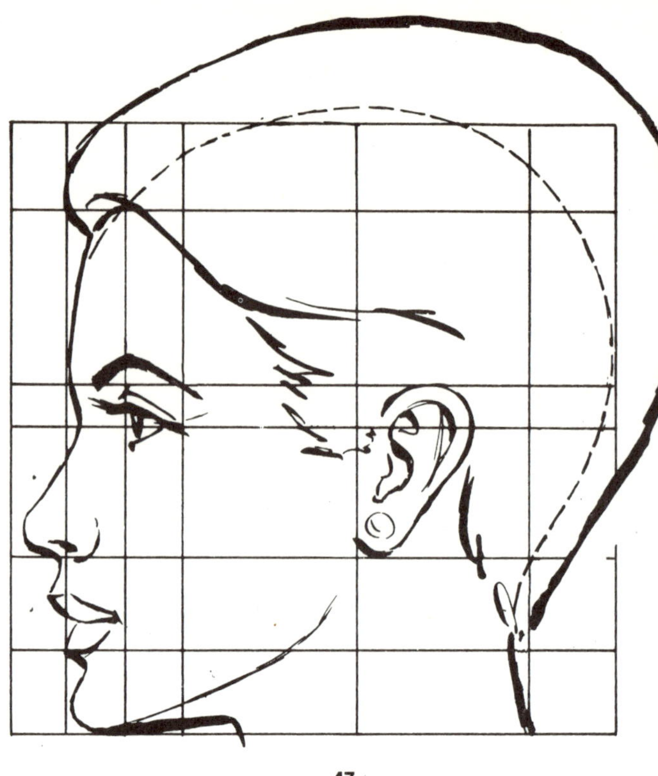

47

A VARIABLE FACTOR

A woman's mouth is slightly smaller than a man's, although the lips are fuller. But, for many years, women have used lipstick to accentuate their lips. In the Thirties fashion was quite the opposite—thin lips and a pinched mouth. Think about the eyebrows of that period. They were very fine, in fact they were sometimes plucked out of existence and a pencil line was drawn instead. Not to mention hairstyles, which go through a complete turnabout every three or four years.

So we must allow for these variables and keep ourselves up-to-date. Generally speaking, an artist needs a quick eye for changing trends and the look of the moment. This is especially vital if he is working in commercial art, where a 'with-it' appearance is absolutely essential.

Examine the drawings on the facing page. They will show you that the technique for boxing up and drawing the head of a woman is the same as for men.

Thus we come to the end of our study of the human head, the perfectly proportioned (and imaginary) head which typifies the ideal.

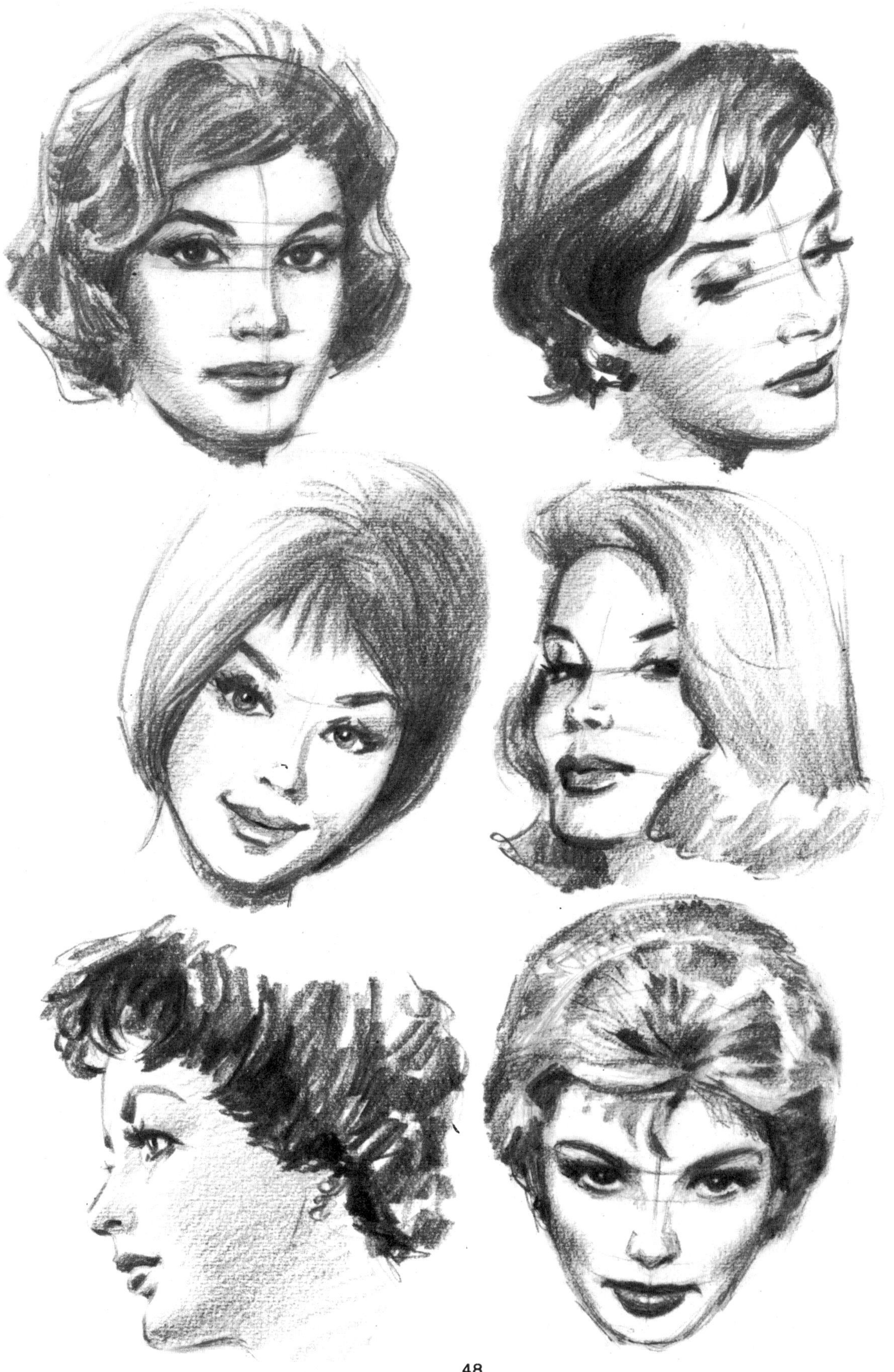

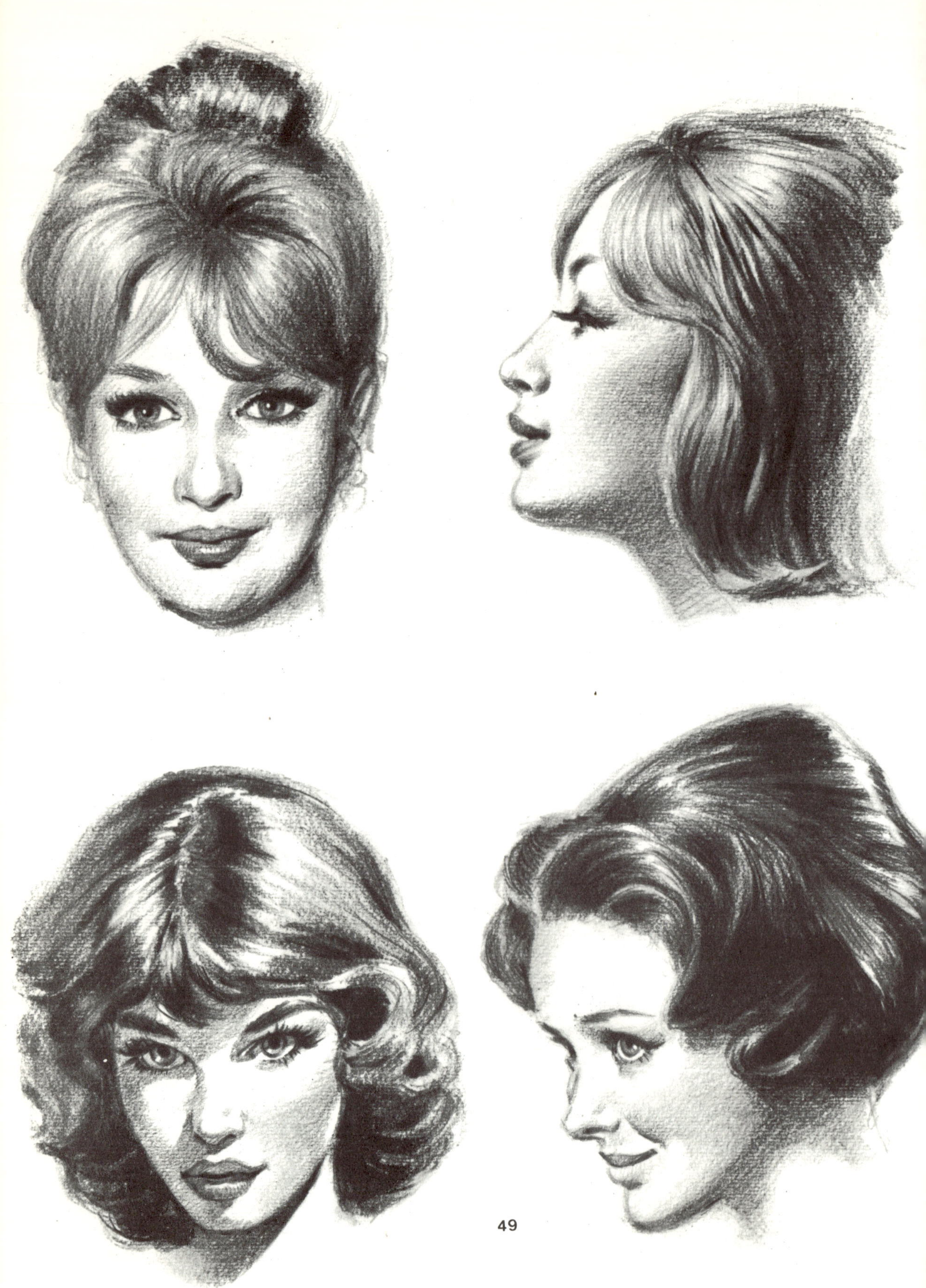

49

A DETAILED STUDY OF FACIAL FEATURES

Eyebrows and eyes - Nose and ears - Mouth

Stand in front of a mirror while you read this and see for yourself what I am talking about. You will never find a model more patient and eager than yourself.

Look in the mirror while you raise, lower and turn your head. Notice the characteristic features of your face.

WHAT COLOUR ARE YOUR EYES?

Do you remember exactly?

(Don't just say that they are light or dark!)

Perhaps you do remember their exact colour... but what about your father, your mother, your brother... what colour are their eyes? What about the friend you see every day? Can you remember? Are his eyes brown, hazel, black, blue, grey, greenish with a blue tint...?

No, I bet you don't remember. Yet eyes are the part of a person's face which you look at most: you look into them whenever you talk to him and when he talks to you.

Our inability to remember this sort of detail means that when studying how to draw eyes —or any other features— we must start by taking a good, hard look at them, imagining that we are seeing them for the first time.

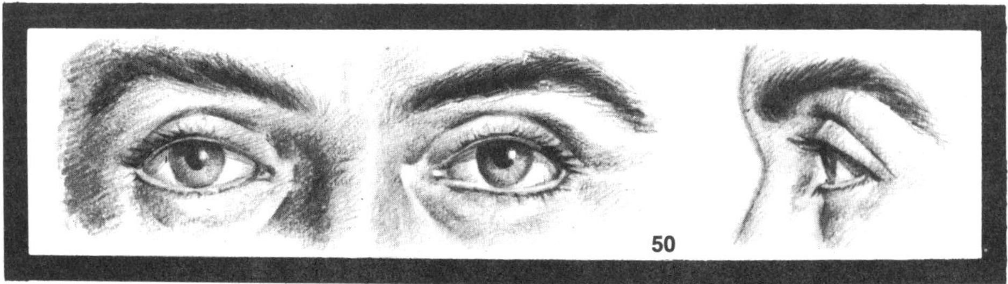

50

Look at the eyes in this illustration for a while (Fig. 50). Don't glance at them as you usually do, casually and inattentively. Study them carefully and examine them in detail.

First, the eyebrows

I know you have seen them before, but this time have a really good look. Eyebrows can be thick or thin, smooth, as if they have just been combed, or shaggy, with thick hairs spoiling their usual shape; they may be arched, almost straight or twisted, etc. (Fig. 51).

When you draw an eyebrow, don't think of it as so many hairs, so many pencil lines... draw the lines in the direction required to imitate the quantity of hairs and the different intensities in tone in the various areas of the brow. Remember that these differences in tone have to be produced by tiny separate lines, not by blending or hatching.

Study the various shapes of the eyebrows when the head is in different positions. Remember that there are two of them, that they are

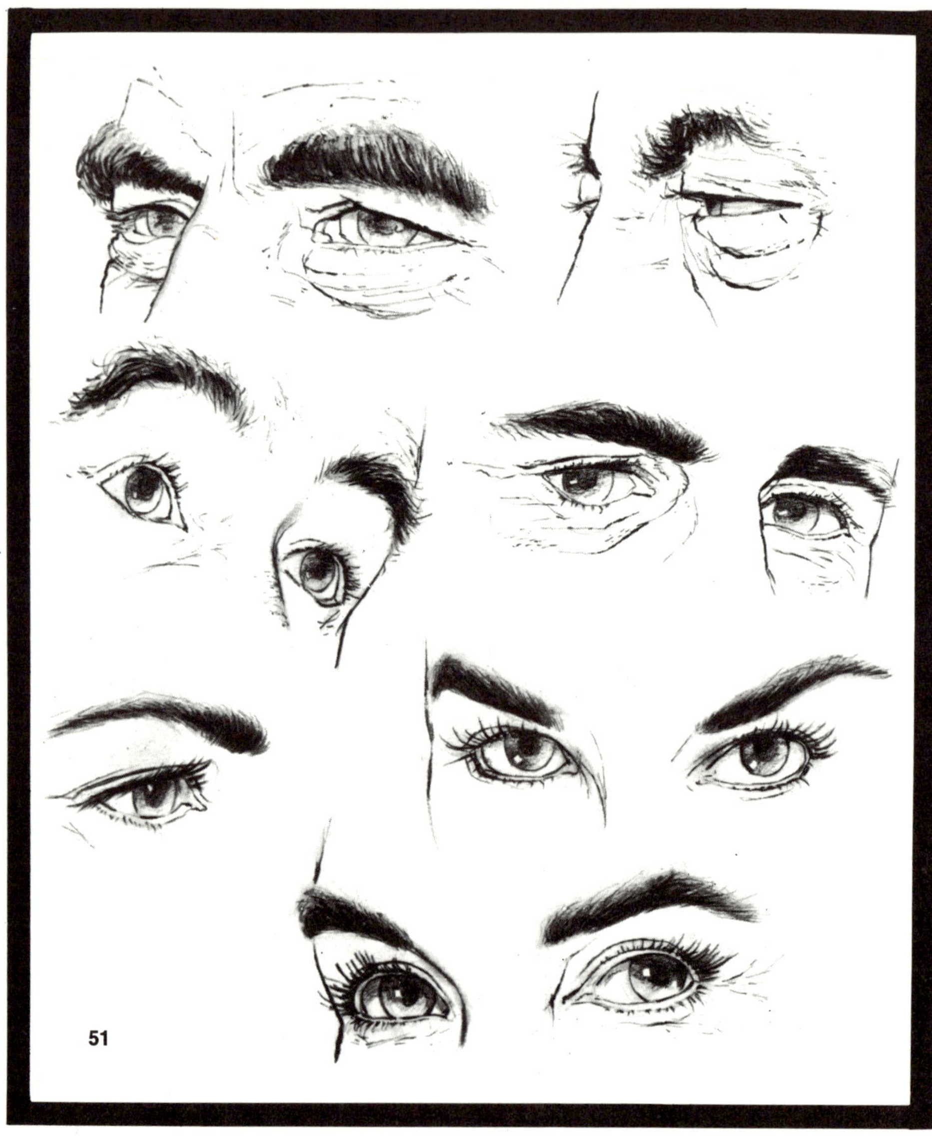
51

symmetrical and lie on a curved surface (the forehead) which curves more at the sides than in the centre.

The eyes are surely the most important and wonderful feature of the human face. There cannot be an artist, a writer, a composer or a poet who has not been inspired at least once by a pair of eyes. Take Matthew Arnold, for example. He put it like this:

«Eyes too expressive to be blue,
Too lovely to be grey».

The outpouring of so much feeling on this subject has led the amateur to believe that he must capture expressiveness, feeling and passion in the lines and shadows of the eyes, so he feels nervous and discouraged, thinking that, to draw eyes properly, he needs the acute perception of a professional.

But don't be put off! You can draw eyes with as much inspiration as you wish, but without filling your mind with preconceived ideas. You must see the eyes for what they really are: small rhomboid shapes with little dark circles inside (the iris and pupil) and a set of tiny curved hairs (the lashes) surrounding them. This means that you must look at them objectively, simply attempting to see their exact shape, colour and tone and the interplay of light and shade. When these basic factors no longer give you difficulty, you can expand a little and express more —but not all that much more— than appears on the surface; but at this stage, please, think only of drawing them as they really are.

Start by looking at and studying just one eye, seen full-face and in profile. Let's have a look at the fundamentals:

VIEW FROM THE INSIDE

As you know, the human eye is shaped like a small sphere —the ocular globe— placed in the bone cavity known as the orbit and covered in front by the folds of skin called eyelids. These can be closed or opened at will, obeying certain muscles which form a ring around the eye.

The main point, as far as we are concerned, is that...

52

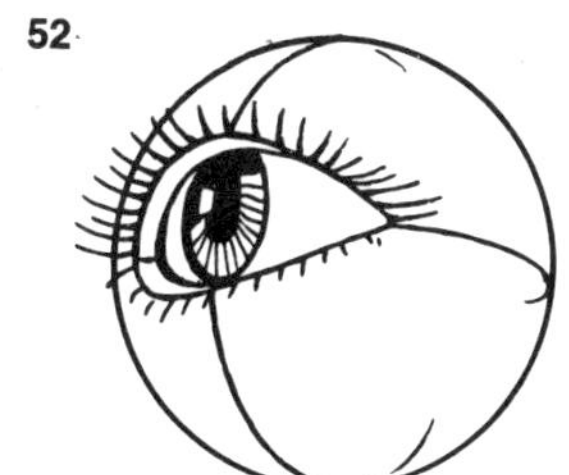

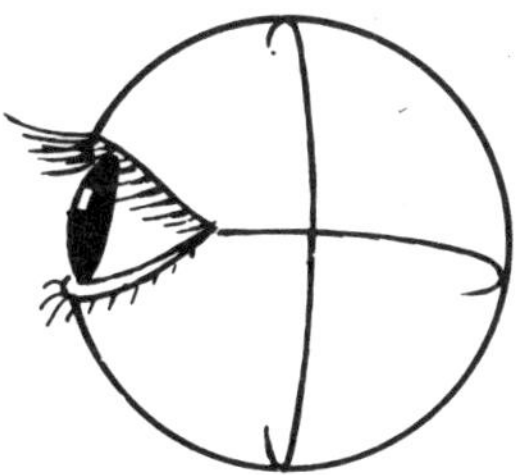

THE EYES ARE SPHERICAL

If we paint a small circle on a marble or similar object and try to draw it from different viewpoints, we come up against the same problems as when we draw eyes —problems of foreshortening and perspective. Try to understand these problems by studying the illustrations on the facing page, noting that the more the marble is turned away, the more foreshortened the circle becomes (Fig. 53).

Imagine the marble with a rubber cover about $\frac{1}{16}''$ thick in which you make a slightly curved slit in which a small dark circle is painted (Fig. 54 *a*).

If we open this slit, we have reproduced the eyelids. Being spherical like the marble, these vary in shape according to their position, but one edge is usually showing (Fig. 54 *b*).

The eyelashes grow out of the edge of the eyelid, forming a right angle with it. Look carefully at the exact point where the lashes start so that you become more aware of their position before drawing them (Fig. 55).

View from the outside

Below the eyebrow is the section of tissue covering the muscles of the upper eyelid. If the skin of the eyelid itself is taut, we can see and draw in the arc it forms (Fig. 56). Otherwise the curved line is partially hidden by the fold of the upper skin. The fold or pouch formed by this tissue can be so pronounced that the shape of the eyelid is completely concealed (Fig. 57).

The eye is closed or opened primarily by the movement of the upper lid. This is lowered like a curtain until it meets the lower lid, which stays put, leaving the upper one to do the work. This helps us to remember a point which is extremely important when we come to draw the open eye:

> *When the eye is open, the curve formed by the edge of the upper lid is longer and more rounded than the curve of the lower lid (Fig. 58).*

So it is usually incorrect to draw an open eye formed by two curved symmetrical lines.

Finally, we must bear in mind that the eyes are set in a curved surface, similar to the forehead, and this curve becomes more pronounced at the sides near the temples (Fig. 59). Therefore, when seen face-on, the eye does not have a symmetrical aperture, as in *a*, but is irregular, as in *b*.

We must also remember the shape and position of the lashes —their roots and how they are placed on the eyelids— and the fact that they lie on a spherical surface; this helps us to understand how they should be drawn from different positions (Fig. 60).

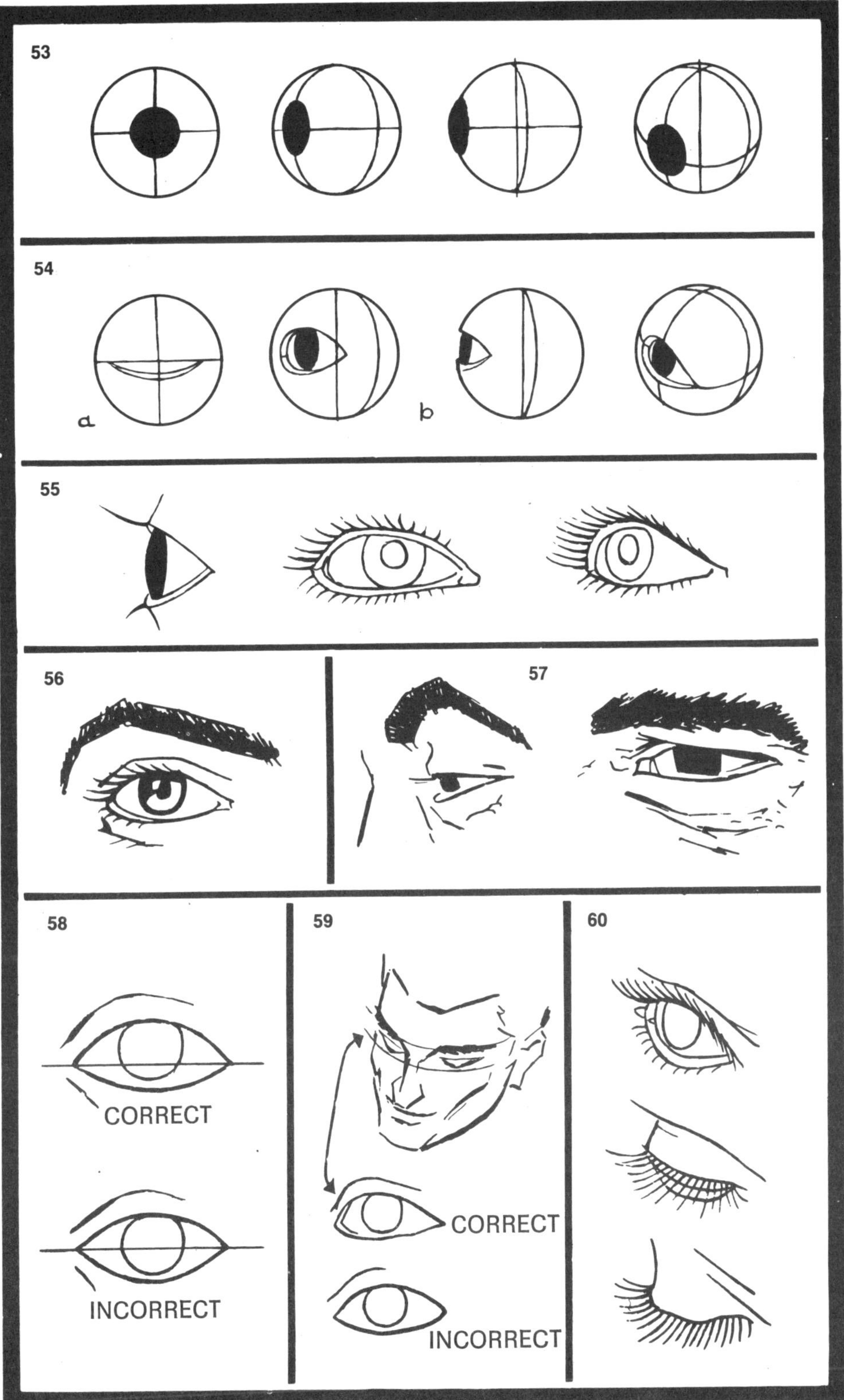
53
54
a
b
55
56
57
58
CORRECT
INCORRECT
59
CORRECT
INCORRECT
60

Let us examine the shapes within the eye, the small circle made up of the iris and pupil. We can then sum up the general characteristics to remember when drawing this feature. (Study the following as if you were actually drawing.)

61

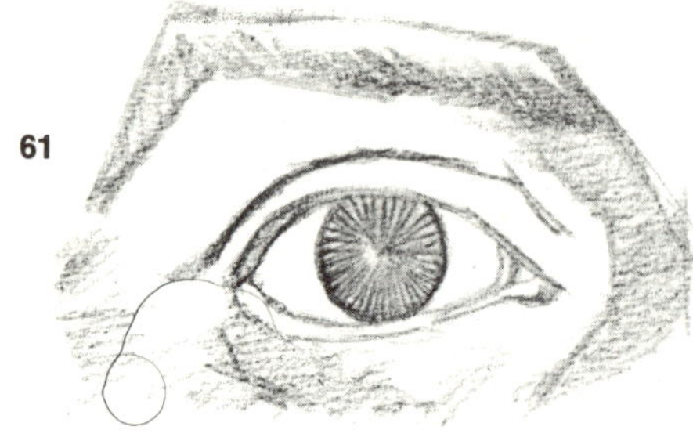

Fig. 61. — Let's forget about the pupil for a moment and imagine the iris as a little circle, with faint lines converging on the centre from the edges. You could leave a space for the highlight at this stage, but we have omitted it here for simplicity's sake.

62

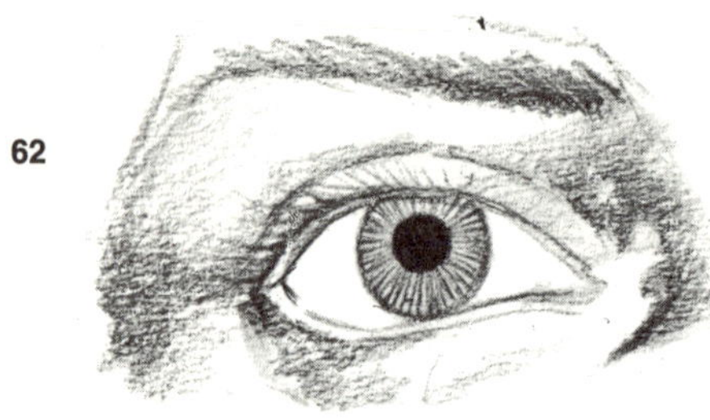

Fig. 62. — We draw a smaller, darker circle inside (in our case, this is nearly always black); this is the pupil.

63—64

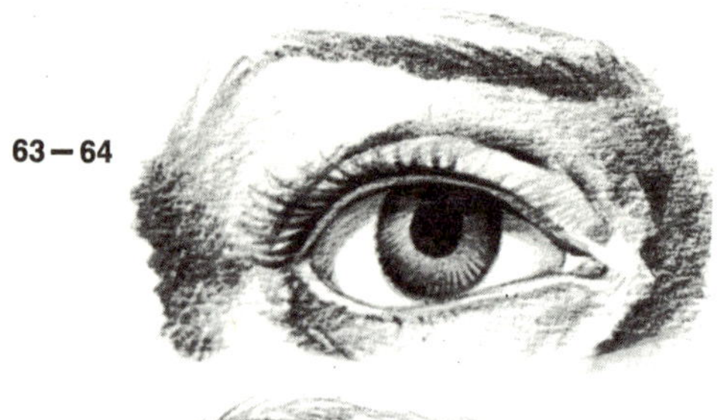

Fig. 63. — There is usually a border of shadow on the upper part of the iris; this is caused by the thickness of the eyelid and lashes.

Fig. 64. — On the left side —or the right, according to the direction of the light— there will be a minute dark patch adjoining a lighter area beside the dark grey circle of the iris.

65

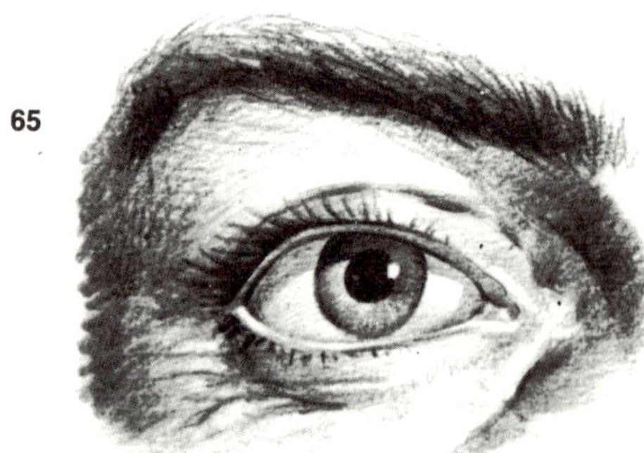

Fig. 65. — On the other side there will also be one or more very small highlights caused by the light. Because the eye is spherical and moist, these are concentrated on one or more points.

All that is left now is the small, pink circle of the tear-gland on the inside of the eye. Fix its size, position and tone in your mind by studying the illustrations, which show it more clearly.

«TWINNING»

Here we have two eyes, moving simultaneously, both set in a curved surface and both spherical in shape... involving every possible problem of viewpoints and duplication (Fig. 66).

The fact that they are on a curve means that we can never see them as two identical features except, of course, when seen absolutely fair and square. But in three-quarter view, for instance, one of the eyes will be seen almost in profile while the other will present a more frontal view.

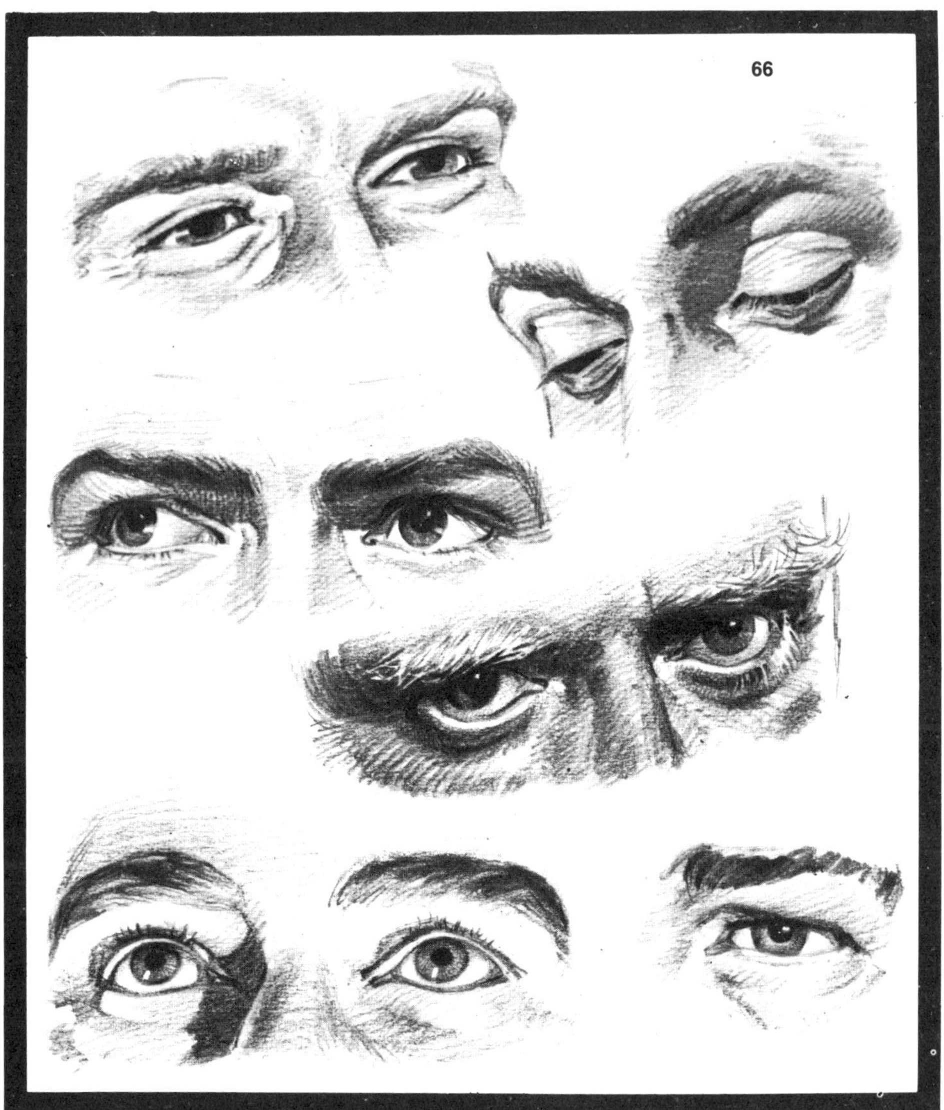
66

This is the basic problem. The only solution is to study very carefully what the model «says» —what the eyes really look like— or when you have to draw from memory, to imagine them as being the two marbles we mentioned earlier.

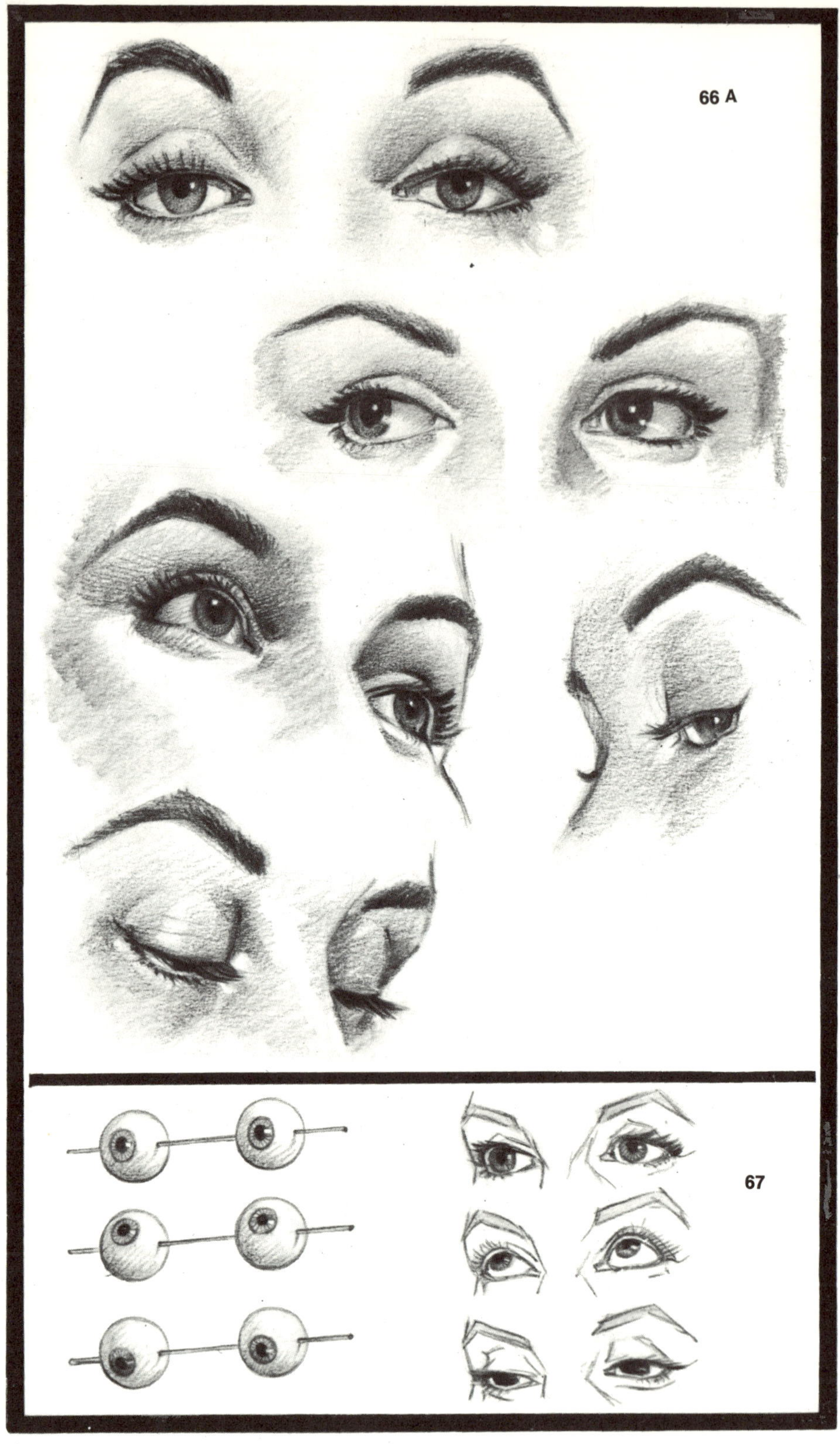
66 A
67

If you can also remember that the two marbles always move simultaneously and that *they are two identical bodies seen from different angles,* it will be almost impossible to produce cross-eyes —the amateur's most common error. It is a matter of simple perspective where the position of one eye determines the position of the other (Fig. 66 A).

This completes our study of the eyes for the time being. Let's move on to the nose and ears.

ANDREYEVITCH *or* ANDRIEYEVITCH?

If you have read the Nobel Prize-winning novel «Doctor Zhivago» by the Russian author Pasternak, I am sure you will agree that it is not a book to be read quickly and casually. This is mainly because of the tremendous amount of material it contains, its profundity, philosophy and poetry. And, also, because of a small detail which at times really got me confused. I mean the fact that the novel includes over a hundred characters, all of whom have Russian names.

So in just the first few pages we encounter Nikolayevna, Kologrivov, Voskoboynikov, Osipovitch, Galaktionovna —and what happens? I think many people read all these names without spelling them out and without noticing whether they are reading about «Andreyevitch» or «Andrieyevitch». Since most of them end in «vitch», «ovski» or «ovna», by the time you get to page 30, you don't know whether Modestovitch is a stationmaster or a canary!

Something like this happens when we draw noses. You fail to see them properly, drawing them badly time and time again because you do not look at them carefully or understand exactly how they are constructed. In profile, they present no difficulty: they are like the name Nadia, which you read and remember at first glance. A three-quarter view is not so bad either, but when it comes to a front view, you have no option but to «spell them out» very slowly, examining the contours and dimensions of the lower section, the areas of light and shade formed by the sides, length and depth of the nose.

To get them right, you must stop yourself seeing them as three-dimensional objects. Look at them carefully as if they were flat,unrelieved shapes with no foreshortening: think of them as a combination of light and shade just as they appear in a painting or photograph.

We can say that, to overcome the foreshortening problem, we need only:

SEE the model without its third dimension

Here's another very important piece of advice:

Try to look at the model as if you had never seen him before

Forget you are looking at a nose: you are merely seeing a collection of areas and you want to get their light and shade down in black and white.

Finally, study the noses drawn on page 49, starting from a simplified shape and drawn from different angles. Look at your nose in a mirror; draw it in one of those positions.

All this also applies to the ears. Who can draw an ear perfectly from memory? We only remember its approximate shape. Study the following illustrations, which show the ear full on, foreshortened, from behind and from the front (Fig. 68).

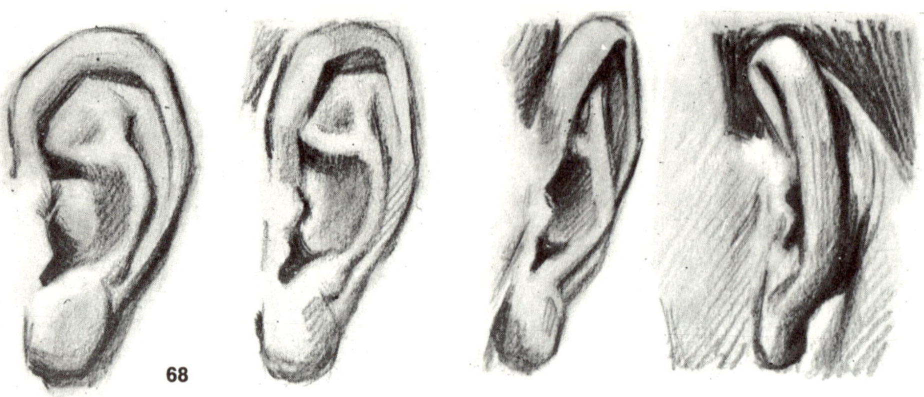
68

Lips and mouth

The Spanish proverb says «No flies enter a closed mouth», but instead of flies we can say «problems»... problems of construction, anatomy and expression. When the mouth is closed, we see just the lips... thick, full, narrow or thin. These have their own perspective since, like the eyes, they lie on a curved surface, with projections, folds, shadows and highlights. Yet to draw a closed mouth is not as simple as it seems.

Look at the mouth in the three-quarters position (a) on the opposite page (Fig. 69), where the side furthest away from us is foreshortened: look at the downward and upward tilt where one lip is more prominent than the other (b) or again, see what it looks like from the front, paying particular attention to the wavy line in the centre (c). Notice the furrows at the side —a strong upward and downward line giving the first hint about character, a person who is always laughing, or someone perpetually dead-pan (d). See how the mouth is given volume by using a lead pencil (this method applies to all techniques, including painting): first, draw a general, fairly uniform tone covering both the highlight and shadowed areas; then, with pencil lines —brush strokes in the case of painting— directed so as to outline the lips and plainly showing the pencil strokes, portray those small vertical ruts, the folded skin of the lips when the mouth is closed (e). Notice that for men the tone is weak and almost imperceptible, while for women it is strong and intense: notice too that feminine lips have a highlight, its shape being marked by pencil lines representing those small ruts (f).

Finally, look at the partly open lips and study their shape. Observe carefully those smooth, fleshy, prominent parts —they can transform the whole shape of the mouth (g).

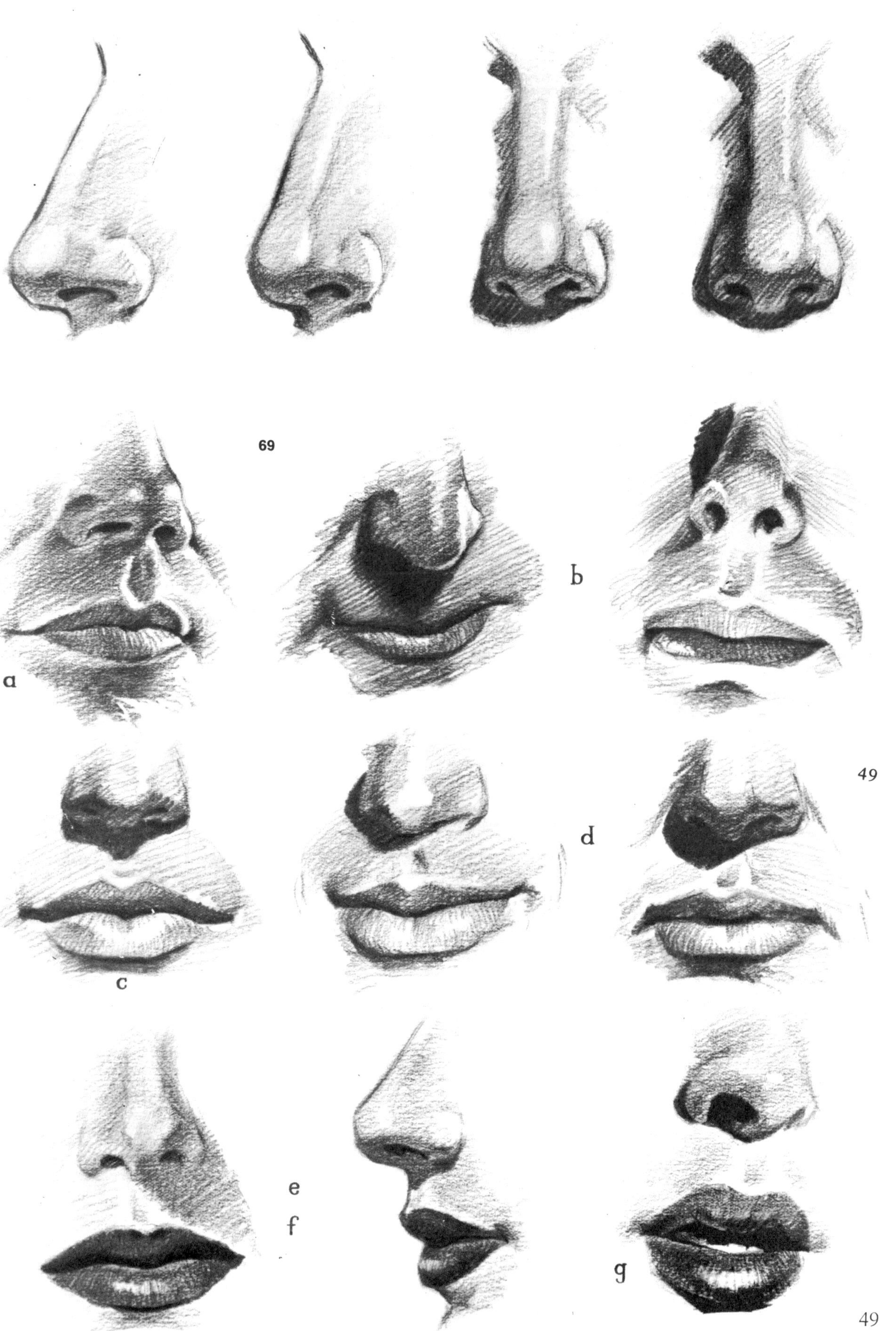
69
a
b
c
d
e
f
g
49

One last piece of advice: when drawing the mouth it is best to include the lower part of the nose and the fold of the chin below the lower lip. These features are closely connected with the shape of the mouth and influence its form, size and general structure.

So far we have only dealt with a closed mouth. Can you imagine what happens when it opens to laugh, smile, shout or cry? The entire face is set in motion: the eyebrows, the eyes, the cheeks, even the sides of the nose. In fact, any movement of the mouth produces a change of expression. We shall leave this subject until later, when we have practised and assimilated what we have learnt so far.

The «trick» used by Raphael and Michelangelo

Talking of «practising and assimilating», I should like to give you a last piece of advice and let you into the secret of Raphael and Michelangelo.

I am already confident that you will be able to draw heads, faces and portraits if you put into practice what you have learnt so far —and I hope you will.

I recommend repeated practice to fix in your mind what I have said about the skull, the basic structure of the head, the perspective of the two «marbles» of the eyes, etc. And I ask you to combine this rather theoretical practice with sketches and drawings from life in front of the mirror, using yourself as the model. For the time being, spend your time drawing isolated features or parts of the face: one eye, both eyes, the nose, etc. Please do not try to draw a complete face; we shall come to that later. Do these drawings as carefully as possible with real eagerness to discover all the shapes facing you in the mirror. In other words:

set down everything as you see it

So we come to the words of Ingres, that master of portraiture, who, when talking with his pupils, revealed the secret of Raphael and Michelangelo:

«Do you know what these great artists did?» he said, «in order to paint and draw those wonderful figures in the Vatican Stanze and the Sistine Chapel? They approached their subjects with awe and reverence; they became humble observers, setting down what they perceived as faithfully and simply as a little child.»

70

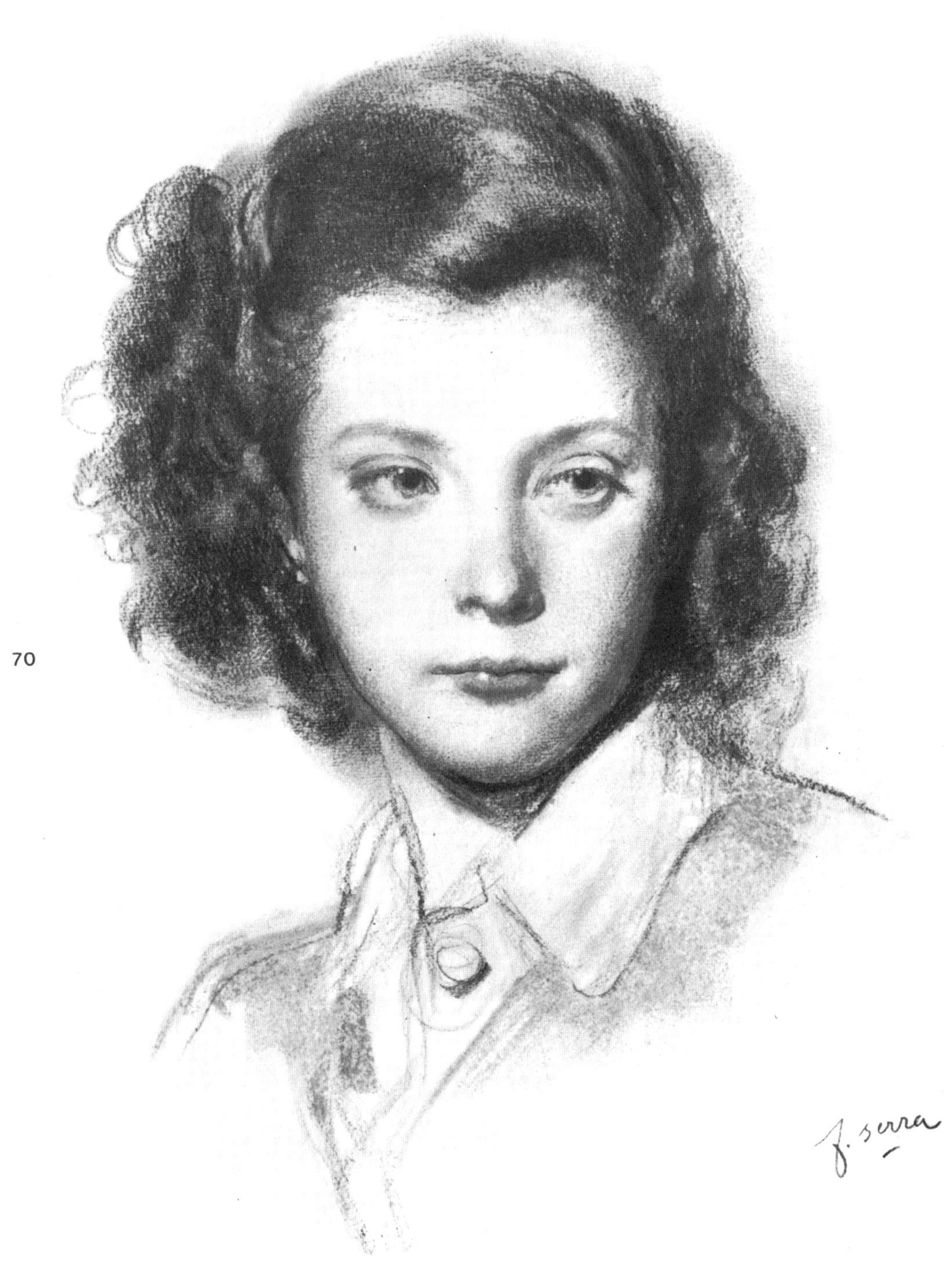

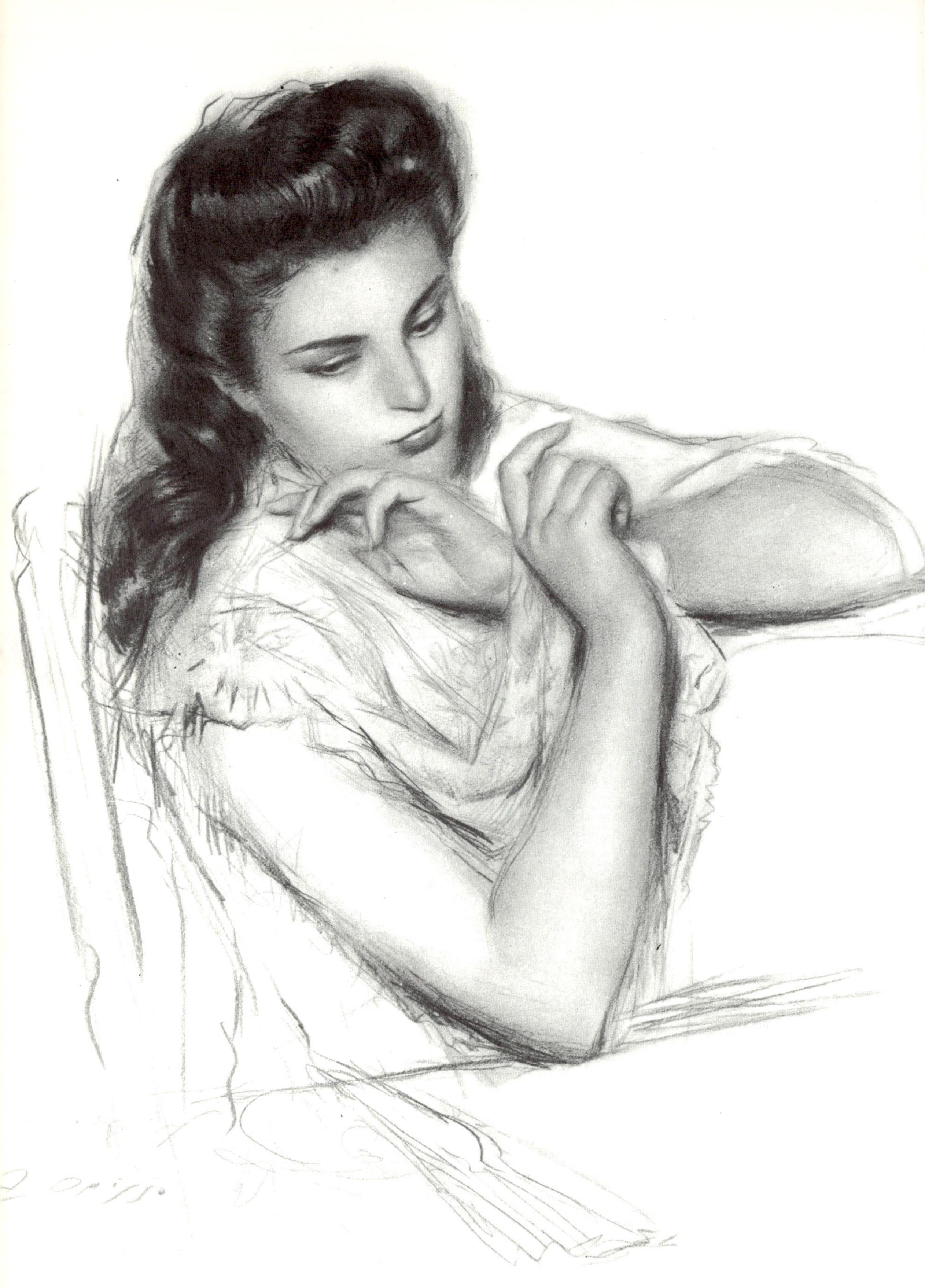

71. Alfredo Opisso. — Pencil portrait.

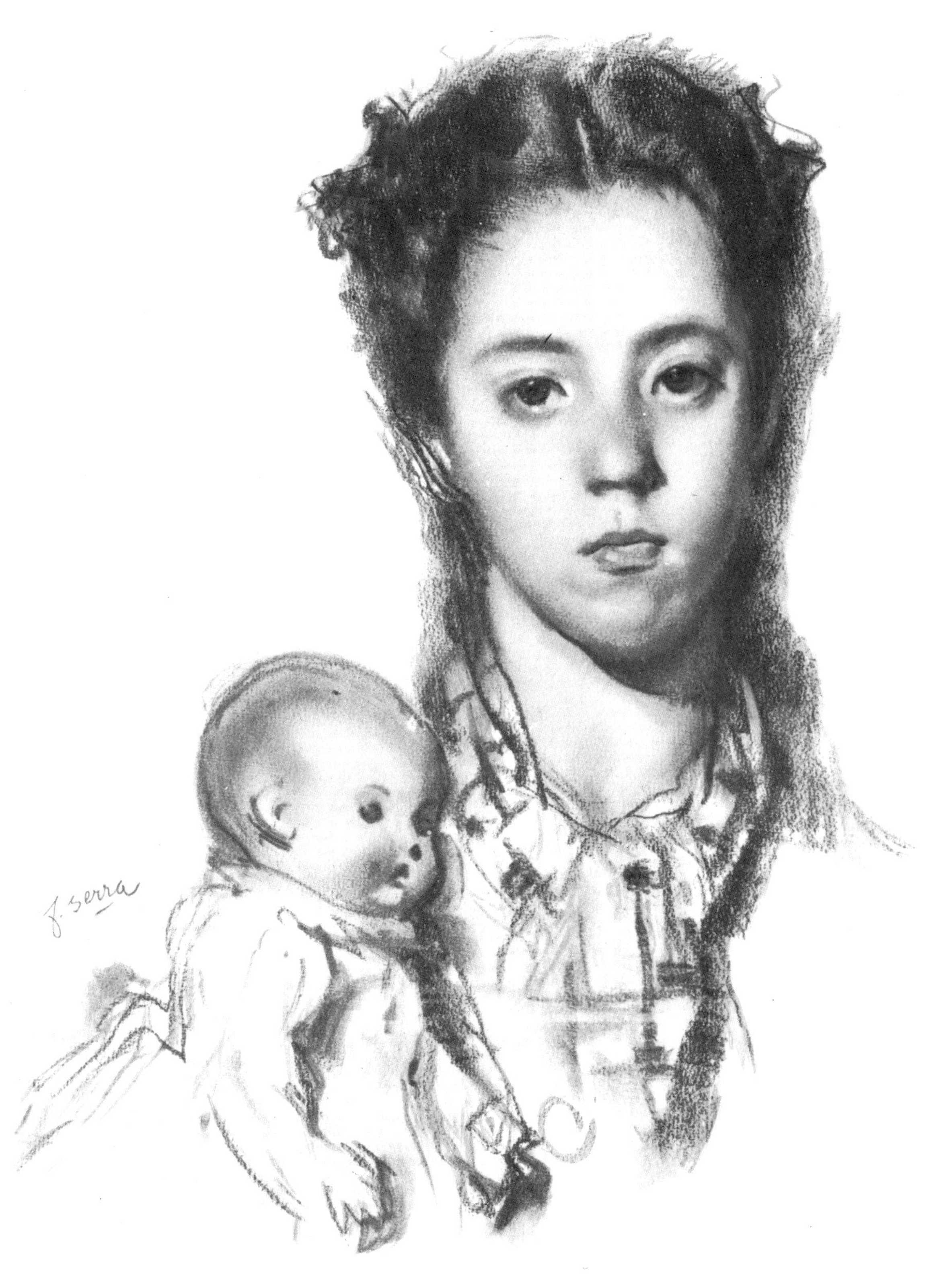

72. Francisco Serra. — Pencil portrait.

PORTRAITS

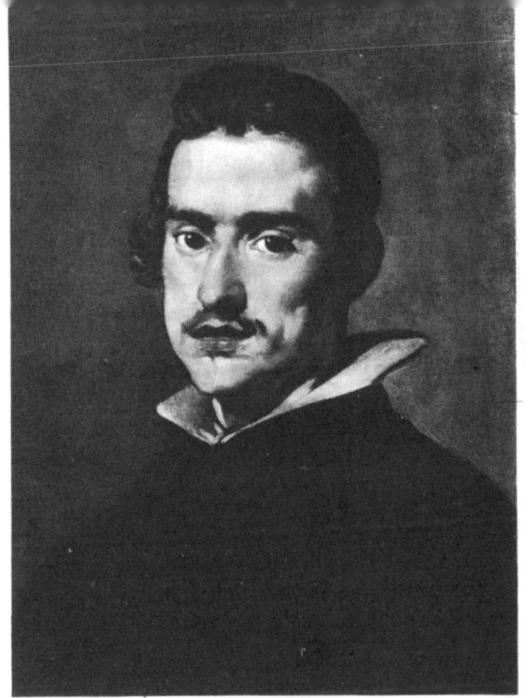

Don Diego Rodriguez de Silva y Velásquez, Court painter to King Philip IV of Spain, was examining his newly completed work, on which the paint was still wet: it was the portrait of Admiral Pulido Pareja. He was alone in his studio, a large room in the Alcazar Palace adjoining the royal apartments.

The King came in: «You still here, Admiral? How are you?»

«The Admiral has left, sire», replied Velásquez, «You are talking to his portrait».

The King came up to the painting with complete amazement.

«Good heavens! I was completely deceived. I thought it was Admiral Pareja in the flesh».

Then, as if wanting to get his own back for the deception, he added:

«Of course... I've heard, Diego, that your skill is simply that you know how to paint a head.»

«You do me an honour in thinking so, Sire, because I do not believe that anyone could paint heads which would deceive Your Majesty.»(1)

THE MASTER'S LESSON

Velásquez's reply to Philip IV is a perfect beginning to this lesson on portraits: it sets us a standard to work by. It proves («You do me an honour in thinking so») that, thanks to his «skill» in drawing and

(1) This anecdote is based upon fact. Velázquez painted the portrait of Admiral Pulido Pareja in 1630. Shortly before that he had exhibited in Madrid an equestrian portrait of Philip IV which caused a sensation and aroused the envy of some of his contemporaries. They criticised the shape of the horse and they said "His skill merely lies in the fact that he knows how to paint a head", just as the King had said.

FIG. 1

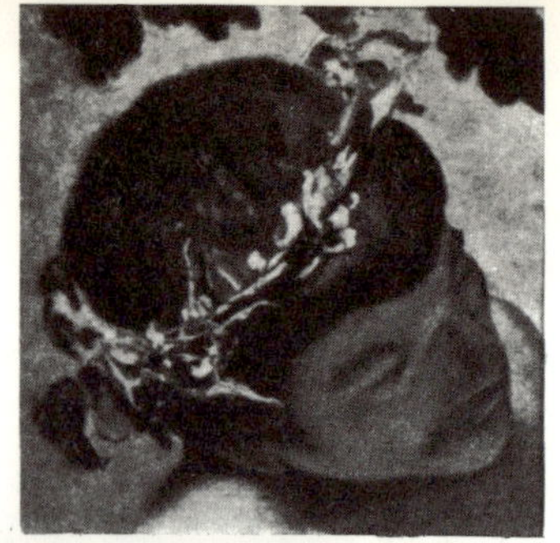

74. The Drinkers

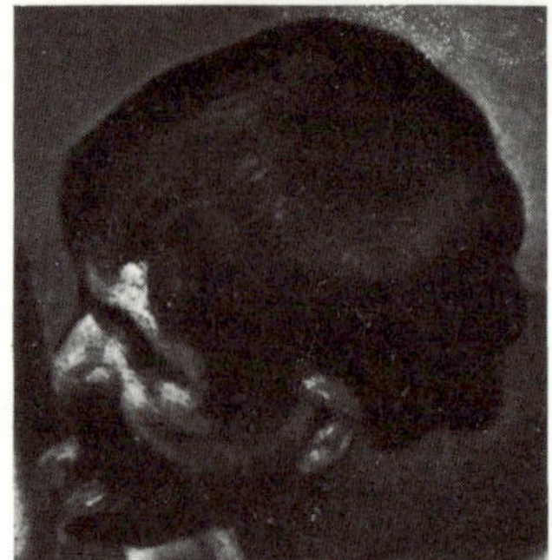

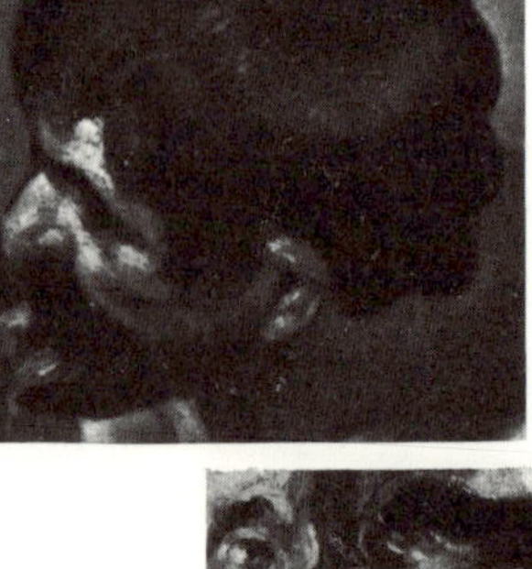

75. Vulcan's Forge

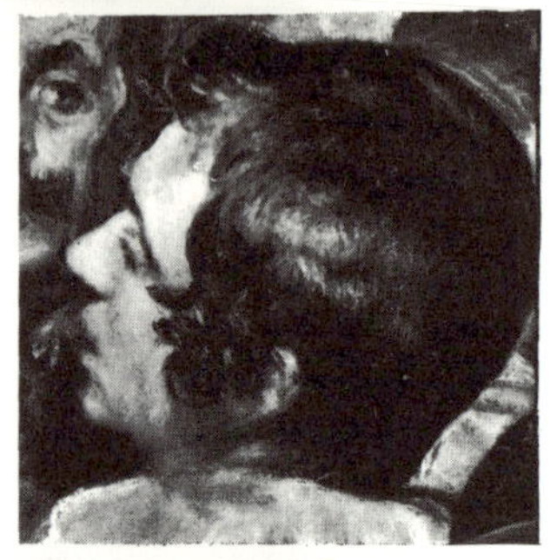

76. The Surrender of Breda

77. Boy from Vallecas

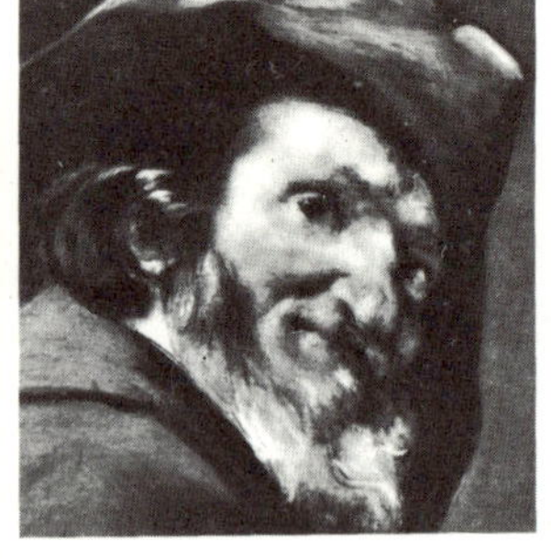

78. Menippus

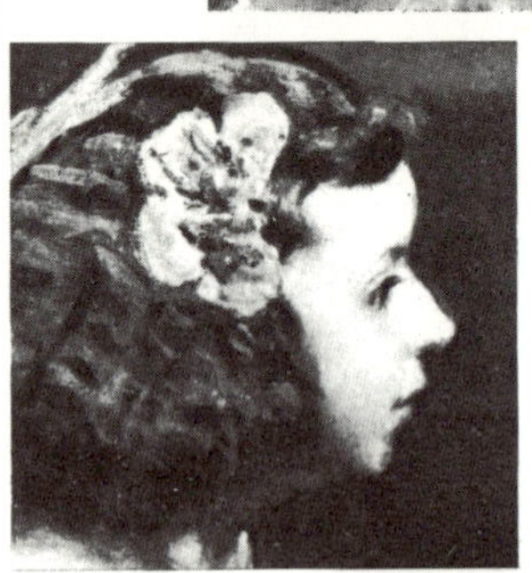

79. Maids of Honour

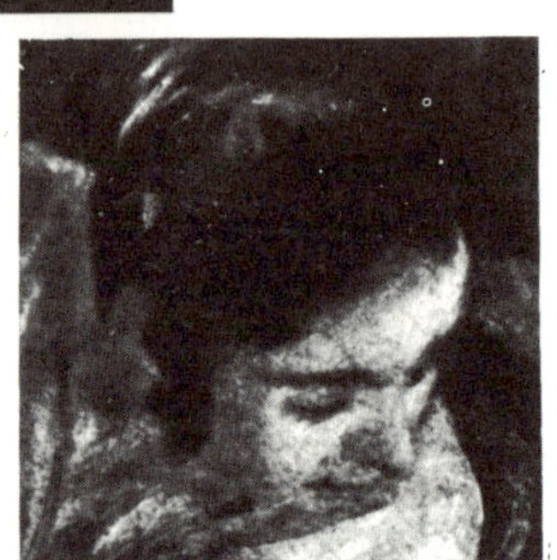

80. The Tapestry Weavers

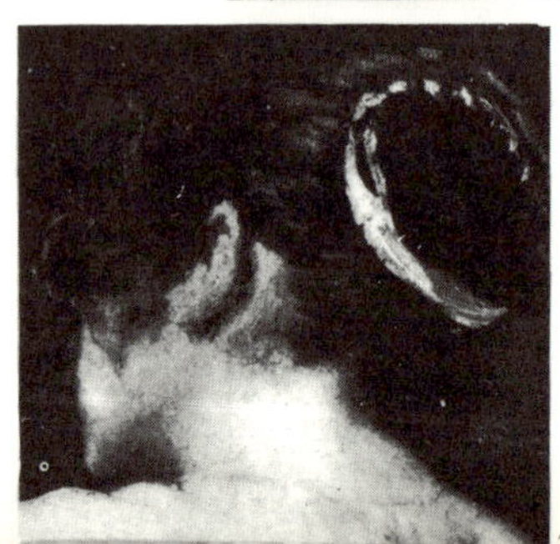

constructing the human head, he could paint a perfect likeness which could deceive even the King.

So that you may understand the significance of this basic aim I suggest you visit the Prado next time you are in Madrid and study the heads which Velásquez painted. First, examine the heads in his paintings of profane, religious, mythological or contemporary subjects, like «The Drinkers», «Vulcan's Forge», «The Surrender of Breda» and «Maids of Honour». (You can see some of these in Figs. opposite). Study, for instance, the difficult foreshortened angle in «Boy from Vallecas» or, even more difficult, the head of «Menippus». What incredible mastery! What sureness of touch, what perfection!

These heads are evidence that Velásquez was a master of portraiture. For one who had clearly solved the problems of drawing and painting the human head with such perfection and could cope with the matter of foreshortening with such mastery and confidence, where was the effort in constructing the human head in a portrait? Non-existent, when we remember that a portrait hardly ever produces a very foreshortened angle and the artist hardly ever paints the head from above or below.

FIG. 2

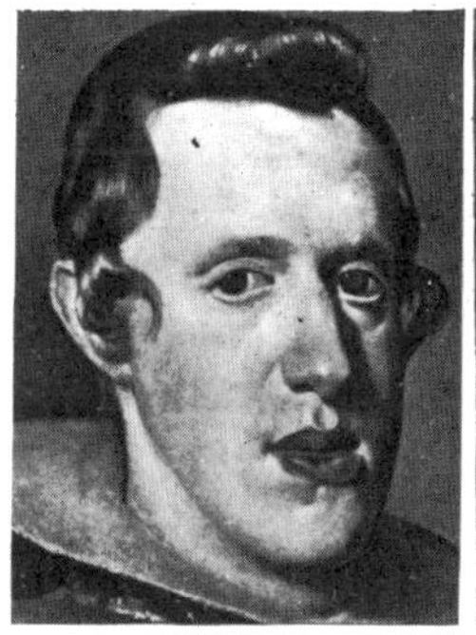

81. Velásquez: Philip IV

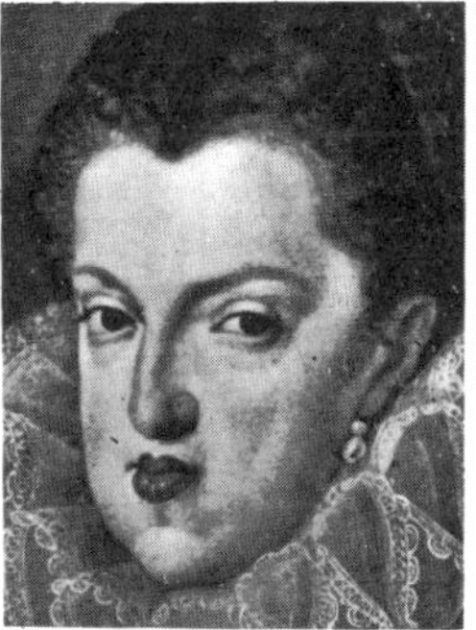

82. Queen Margareta of Austria

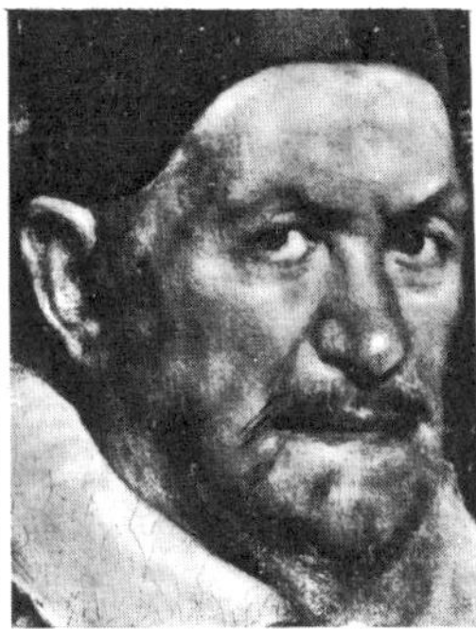

83. Pope Innocent X

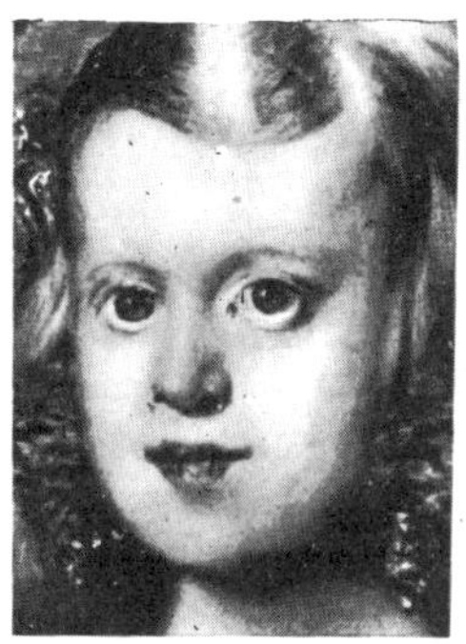

84. The Infanta Margareta of Austria

Portraits presented no problem to Velásquez. Getting the eyes of Queen Margareta of Austria at the right level and the right size, for example, or keeping the nose, mouth and chin in the symmetrical centre of the face, forming the oval of the face and showing it in three-quarter view without raising or lowering the head; for Velásquez all this must have been as easy as drawing a straight line, done in a flash almost without thought. And obviously, if it was no effort for him to construct a head, *then he could devote his attention to the more elaborate and subtle aspects of portrait painting;* he could concentrate, for example, upon emphasising the most individual traits of the model, trying to obtain the «perfect likeness», the closest representation of his subject, so that the subject would appear to be living, speaking, watching him, just like Admiral Pareja, who seemed to be present «in the flesh».

So... Velásquez teaches us this:

The basic essential for a good portrait is a complete mastery of the construction of the human head

Remind yourself of this again and again. You should acquire at the outset a firm grasp of the rules and instructions given in the first part of this manual. You should know the canon of proportions by heart, the peculiarities of all the different parts of the face —eyes, nose, mouth, ears, hair, etc.— the data on bone structure and expression, the changes wrought by age and the dissimilarities between the male face and the female.

With all this information stashed away, you can move on to this section, which provides basic instructions in portraiture.

FUNDAMENTALS OF A GOOD PORTRAIT

There are two fundamental requirements for every good portrait. This section will be devoted to them.

1) The portrait must be an exact likeness of the subject.

2) It must in itself be a work of art.

The first speaks for itself: if it is not a likeness, it is not a portrait. However, the term «exact likeness» involves a number of physical and psychological factors which, as we shall see, are not as easy to deal with as they may at first appear.

The second condition means that the portrait must be admired and accepted as a work of art, regardless of whether it is a good likeness. In other words, likeness is not everything. Passport photographs resemble the subject, but that's about all — they have no artistic merit. But every day thousands of people admire portraits like the one of Pope Innocent X by Velásquez (Fig.83), not because of its likeness to the subject —nobody is bothered about that— but because of its intrinsic value as a work of art.

Let us now study the criteria by which these two essentials are judged. But before we go on, please read «Ingres' advice to his pupils» (p. 59). These notes were found in a notebook by a descendant of one of the French artist's pupils. The maxims were propounded during conversations in the studio about the art of portraiture and figure drawing in general. They remain valid for ever and are absolutely relevant to our subject.

You will find some of Ingres' precepts in this section, but it is worth reading them in full now — refer back to them again and again. You cannot afford to ignore them.

Ingres' advice to his pupils

We must capture the caricature, the essence of everything we see. In order to discover that caricature, a painter needs to be a physiognomist.*

The good artist must penetrate the mind of the model.

Grasp the uniqueness of your model - he is not just a strong man, he is a Hercules.

Study the model's most characteristic pose. The body should not follow the movement of the head. First note the natural physiognomy of your model; position him accordingly, let him express himself naturally.

Examine the model 'in depth' before you begin.

No two persons are alike; give each every bit of his individuality.

Sketching is the art of grasping the character, the dominant trait, in the face, the mind of the subject.

Study and observe the poses characteristic of each age group. In movement, there is always one profile more significant than the other.

The artist at work must be ever watchful, ever mindful of detail, right up to the last moment.

Draw the eyes as you go - don't leave them till the end.

One paints as one draws.

Try to put some life into the dark areas.

It is not white which first meets the eyes; it is the medium shades, the deep shadows.

Details are great gossips; muzzle them.

Note the limits of the shadows, the medium shades and the highlights.

Avoid too many highlights - they can spoil the effect.

Portraits of women need as much light as possible.

Breathe vitality into the figure.

Build on a basic concept, continually seeking, uniting, comparing. See how art develops. Look first of all at Michelangelo, then look at Raphael, who owed everything to Michelangelo. Both artists reached perfection by giving themselves up to their craft, by submerging their egos, by faithful representation.

* A person who has the art of judging character from features of face or form of body.

A PERFECT LIKENESS

Right from the beginning make a distinction between two general factors which determine what we call «a perfect likeness».

We can then sub-divide these two general factors as follows:

PHYSICALLY, the likeness is determined by:

a) *A scientific approach to constructing the head.*

b) *A conscious exaggeration of the subject's main characteristics.*

PSYCHOLOGICALLY, the likeness is produced through:

aa) *Expression.*

bb) *Demeanour and pose.*

Don't be alarmed at beginning with all these rules.You will see how the crux of each can be grasped and learnt quite simply. Let us begin by studying the physical factors:

DRAWING THE HEAD — A SCIENTIFIC APPROACH

> *«Build on a basic concept, continually seeking, uniting, comparing.»*
>
> Ingres

By scientific approach, we mean boxing-up, precise calculating, accurate positioning, exact proportions. We mean, in fact, making a perfect replica of what is before us. If we cannot do that, all our rules are worthless.

INTENTIONAL EXAGGERATION OF THE SUBJECT'S MAIN CHARACTERISTICS

> *«Everything we see has a caricature which we must capture. To discover that caricature a painter must be a physiognomist.»*
>
> Ingres

Taking the scientific, photographic construction of the model's head as a base, we must concentrate on the most characteristic features, discover which they are and emphasise them, exaggerating them slightly in order to make the likeness more perfect. This is something the artist can do only by using his creativeness and his technical skill; no camera can capture it.

As Ingres said, we must discover and pinpoint the caricature which is always there. What is the model really like? Are his eyes large, small, close together, wide apart? Heavy eyebrows? Is his face round, drawn, bony, broad? Oddly enough, our perception of physical characteristics is usually based upon descriptions and mental images which, in essence, are perfect caricatures. When trying to describe something, our brain does, as it were, «draw a caricature».

For instance, look at these photographs of two great men, General de Gaulle and the ill-fated President Kennedy. (Fig. 85)

85

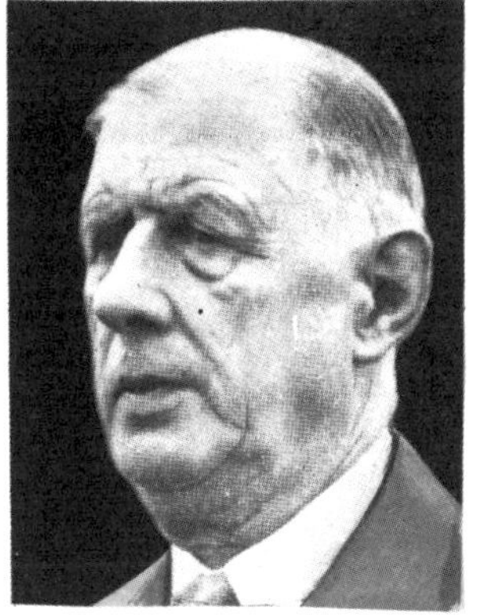

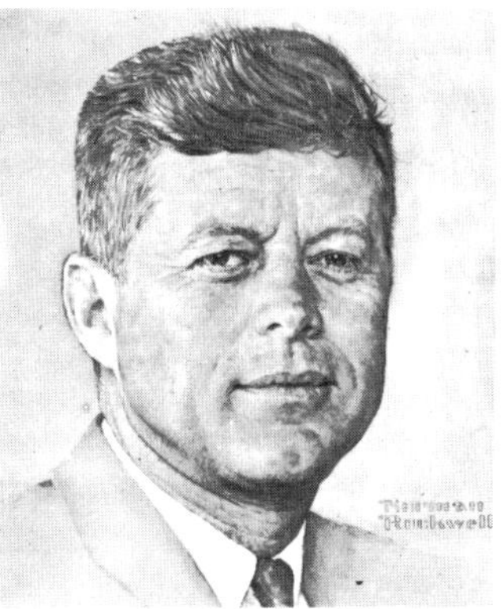

You recognise them, of course. Can you tell me how you recognise them? How do you recognise the portrait on the left as General de Gaulle and the one on the right as President Kennedy?

«Well... because de Gaulle has a big nose, long face, large ears... and Kennedy, on the other hand, has a short nose, small ears and square face». That's your brain «drawing a caricature». Look at this:

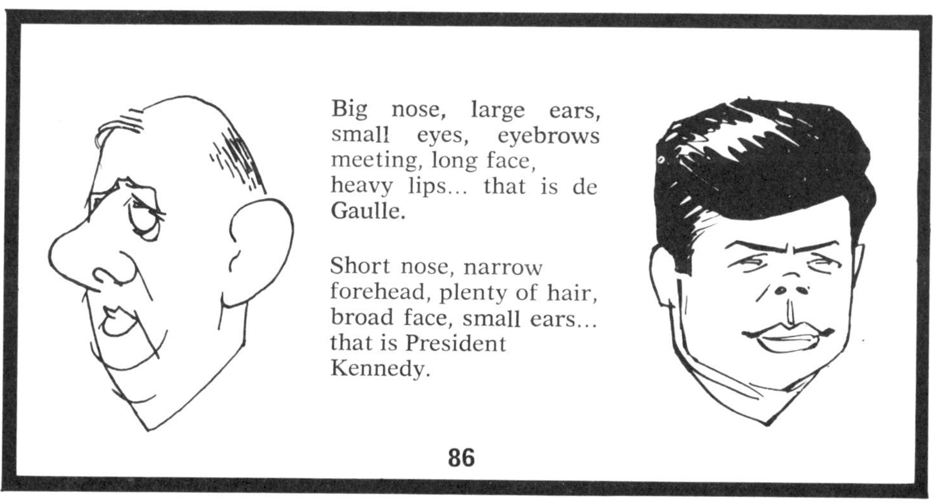

86

Kennedy, de Gaulle, you and I, we all have our characteristic features. All we have to do is to recognise them clearly, observe them, assess them, compare them with our own and other people's so that we can judge how high, long, narrow or broad they are. We can then exaggerate them slightly, in order to get down on paper what other people see — this is the way to get the perfect likeness.

Facial expression and pose of the model

«Study the pose of the head and body. First note the physiognomy of your model, then position him accordingly.»

Ingres

We all have a characteristic expression and pose which are as much part of us as the colour of our skin and the tone of our voice. Ken always bends his head a little when talking; John has a habit of peering over his spectacles; Sally looks as if she has a stiff neck. When she moves her head, her body usually moves with it as if they were all of a piece. One person tends to tilt his head upwards when looking at something; another stretches his neck; someone else again is highly strung and his attitude and expression look a little unnatural.

Some people seem more peculiarly themselves when seen in full-face, rather than in three-quarter view. Others present more character in profile.

Ingres portrayed Napoleon in typical pose, left arm bent so that his hand was inside his jacket, a posture so characteristic that it says one word —«Bonaparte». Pope Pius XII was often painted in profile— do you remember? Presumably because it was in his profile that his dignified humility and brilliance really showed through. Finally, we have the example of General de Gaulle. I do not have a portrait of him in front of me, but I think that the best way to depict him would be with head slightly raised, in that position which was so typical of him and which we have seen so often in photographs and newsreels, a product of his military background and his great pride in everything French, personified in himself.

The model's expression and pose are part of himself. What we have to do is allow him to be himself.

Features express character

The good artist must penetrate the mind of the model.

Ingres

The final component of a true likeness is the model's own character.

What sort of person is he? We must try to get him right. Is he cheerful, confident, determined or pessimistic, withdrawn, indecisive? What does his face tell us? What do we know about him? Character is often reflected in the face —it is the mirror of the mind. The shape of the lips, prominence of the jawbone, lines around the mouth, the pouches under the eyes and actual expression —remember what you have learnt— all this sometimes enables a good artist to «read» the model's character.

So you must observe those character-revealing traits and keep them in mind when you come to draw the portrait; exaggerate them a little to express the model's personality and produce an even better likeness.

From this character-study you may arrive at a special pose for the head or a particular type of lighting which emphasises the model's impulsive, ingenuous, optimistic, reserved or open temperament, etc. But we shall deal with this later when we put these instructions into practice.

At this point, remember that to get a perfect likeness, you must:

Construct the head correctly, revealing its characteristics, pose it suitably and convey its individuality.

Ingres gives us a piece of advice which sums up the correct approach. Please look at it carefully — I consider it especially relevant to this section. Like many of his recommendations, it is full of good sense and meaning, which can be interpreted in many ways. He says:

EXAMINE THE MODEL 'IN DEPTH' BEFORE YOU BEGIN

«Examine»; what does he mean? Perhaps find out if the model is comfortable or whether he has been drawn before? No, what Ingres meant is quite clear. He meant:

GET TO KNOW THE MODEL

familiarise yourself with his features and gestures, chat with him and put him at his ease. Allow him to be himself, to show what he is really like.

Of course, this must be done in conversation, making him feel at home. But don't you agree that it can also be done by drawings, preliminary sketches which enable us to seek out his quintessence, as it were, as if each sketch were posing a question? This is the way to do it. These preliminary sketches are essential; they will help you to work out the final portrait, asking yourself whether any of the drawings show the ideal position, the absolutely right lighting, that lightning flash of recognition which produces a perfect likeness.

These rough sketches will also give you a chance to sharpen your creative imagination by considering vital aspects of the work, like composition, the interplay of light and shade, the treatment and the style...

A WORK OF ART

THE TECHNIQUE OF PORTRAIT DRAWING

The instructions given in the previous pages apply to portraits whether *drawn* or *painted*. In either case the artist must make use of the ingredients we have mentioned which are necessary for a perfect likeness. But from the artistic point of view, leaving aside the question of likenesses, drawing is a very different matter from painting. In a pencil portrait, for instance, artificial lighting is preferable for reasons which we shall study later; concentration upon the centre of interest —the head— can be obtained quite differently in pencil portraits as compared with paintings; the background is determined by the medium and in drawings it will usually be white; the size of the picture and the figure itself are smaller in drawings than in paintings, and so on. For these and other reasons the instructions given below refer to pencil portraits only.

For convenience, we shall arrange the subject matter in the order which the artist would use. From the artistic point of view, the first thing to consider is the type of light, its direction and quality.

LIGHTING

Artificial lighting is generally used for a *drawn portrait*. It can be produced by one 100 watt or two 60 watt bulbs; in the latter case one bulb lights the model and the other the drawing board.

Francisco Serra, an expert in pencil portraits, uses one 100 watt bulb to light the model and the drawing board. Alfredo Opisso, also famous for his pencil portraits, prefers to use two. But these preferences are not all that important. What is important is that all the experts use artificial light for this kind of work.

Why? For three good reasons: first and foremost because, when drawing, they do not bother about colour, but only light and shade, black and white; secondly, because artificial light is a «directed», firm light which therefore «models» the subject more satisfactorily, bringing out more clearly the features and prominent traits; thirdly, because artificial light can be moved around as necessary. (Also, of course, artificial light has the advantage of allowing the artist to work at any time).

THE MOST FAVOURABLE DIRECTION

There is no difference of opinion about this. For a drawn portrait the best direction is from the side in front of the model but more frontal than lateral. There is certainly no point in projecting broad, heavy

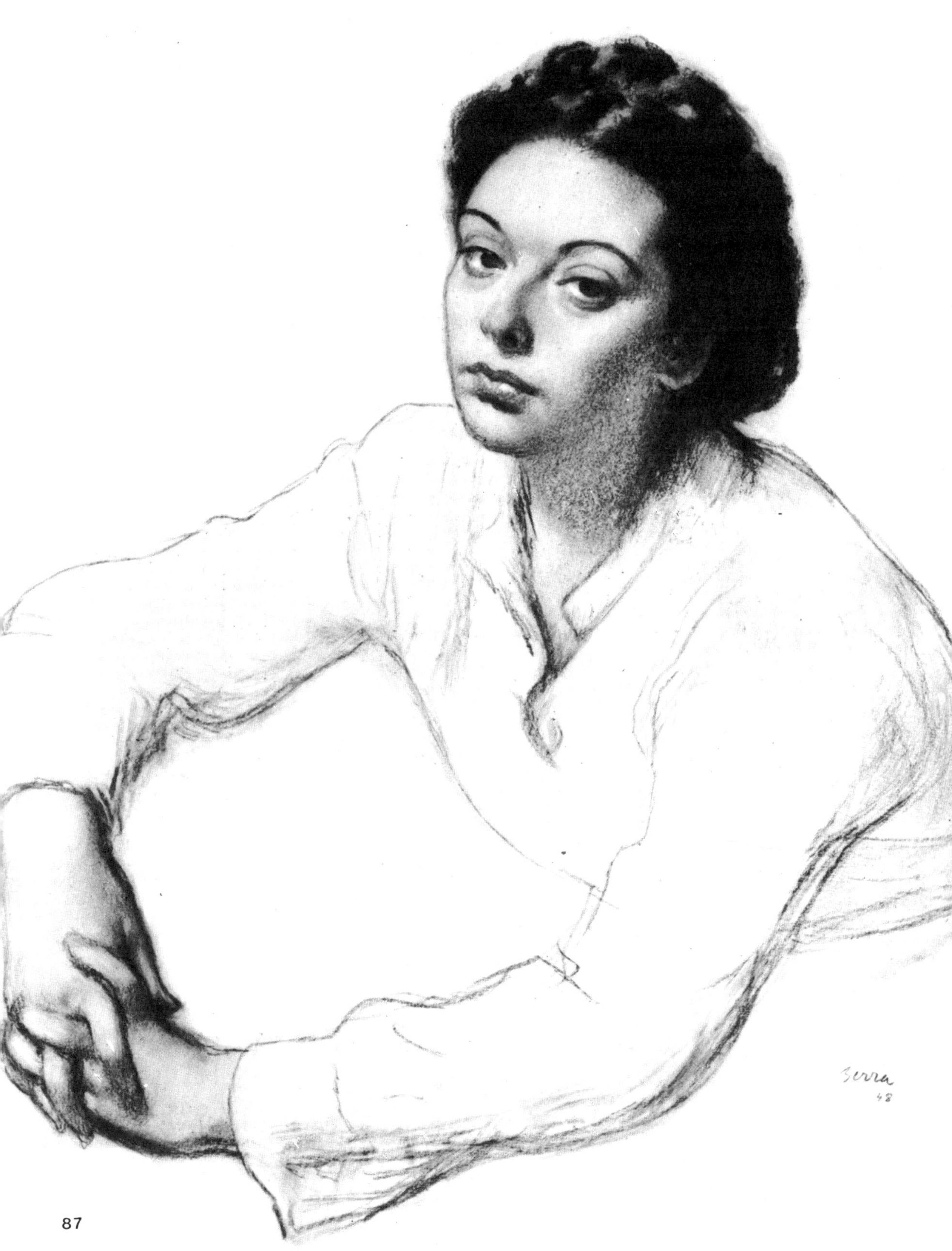

87

shadows which make the drawing more complex. It is not a question of dramatising emotions or passions, but simply of portraying, of explaining who and what the model is, of, to use Ingres' expression, capturing his caricature. And we have already seen how a caricature can be produced even without light or shaded areas, simply by using lines.

The modern portrait has more light than shadow.

To get this idea across in one sentence:

Lighting should illuminate the model from an almost frontal direction, slightly above and to the side of the model's head.

88

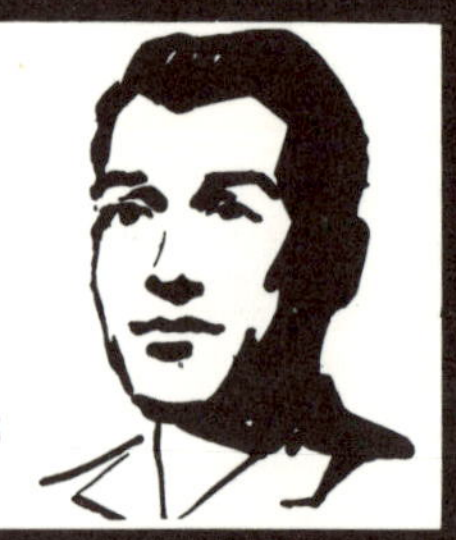

Only slightly above and to the side so that the nose projects its shadow strongly downwards, but laterally enough to produce a shadow on one side of the face, the side nearest the artist. Study the example given in Fig. 88 above.

There can be no hard and fast rule about this — it should be adapted to the physiognomy, character, age and sex of the model. There is no one lighting method which can be used for every portrait. That would be like working with one of those photographic booths which provide passport photographs: you enter, the light goes on, goes out... someone else enters, the light goes on, goes out... and so on. This would make a nonsense of everything I have said about likenesses. Notice the direction of the lighting in the portraits illustrating this book (pp. 51, 52, 53, 65, 81, 83 and 85). Compare the heads and see how they differ. Note the different treatment of the shadowed areas for men and women: this is extremely important with regard to the lighting and the interpretation of the treatment.

We are not cameras

On the subject of treatment and its interpretation, we have to remember that *the quality and quantity of artificial light remain constant.* It always produces the same luminosity and rather clear-cut, hard areas of light and shade, which also remain constant, regardless of whether the model is male or female. Constant quality and quantity of light is usually disastrous in photography; a photograph of Margaret, a chic, delicate-featured girl, has the same contrasts and qualities as a photograph of Ted, a hefty chap who knows how to throw a javelin and toss a caber.

But we are not cameras! We can and must vary our approach, use hard or soft lines, vary the shading, make the areas of light and shade clear-cut or soft, depending upon whether the model is strong or weak, a man or woman, a child or a pensioner.

Have another look at the portraits we have used as illustrations; compare the treatment of the different faces; notice the interpretations used for a woman's face as compared to a man's. They are different, aren't they? Each face has been given its own distinct treatment. That is what you must do when you have the model in front of you. Don't just copy the values and contrasts the model gives you; interpret them in your own way and adapt your interpretation to the model's character, age, sex, etc.

Having arranged the light and the model and found the most suitable type of lighting, the artist then begins to consider the pose.

THE POSE

If you are drawing the head only, the model must be seated. If the portrait is to be half-length, he can sit or stand, although contemporary style usually shows him seated. In any case, his head should be level with your own. Remember this important rule:

The model's eyes must be level with your own.

THE MODEL MUST BE COMFORTABLE

For instance, get him to sit down and make himself as comfortable as possible so that he can hold the pose as long as necessary without getting tired or fed up.

Above all, watch out for that unnatural rigidity which is typical of people who are too self-conscious. Sometimes we have to distract the model, chat with him until he relaxes.

NORMAL CLOTHING, NORMAL HAIRSTYLE, ETC...

Francisco Serra told me once: «It is a terrible mistake to draw a young man dressed up in his best suit, beautifully pressed shirt and neatly knotted tie.»

The stiffer the clothes, the less suitable they are for our purpose. For example, a woman's dress straight out of the shop window is not as flexible as one that has been worn; it lacks those soft folds and creases which are naturally adapted to the person's figure. A new suit is like armour-plating; it has no fluidity or movement and seems as cold and lifeless as it does on the dress-maker's dummy.

Avoid brand-new clothes if you can. For example, dress a school boy in a sweater or a young girl in an everyday blouse, and so on.

Never draw a man, woman or child with an unnatural hairstyle. Mothers sometimes dress their children up to the nines, plastering them with haircream and lacquer —«because they are going to see the painter». This can completely destroy the effect. «Leave them as they are», Serra says to the mother, «just as they are when they get home from school; hair flopping over the forehead, ordinary sweater and everyday trousers; *that is the real child*». («Heavens above», say the mothers, «people will think we haven't anything else for them to wear».)

«Express the truth, but judiciously»

Obviously, if the child's sweater has a tear, leave it out: if it is very crumpled, do not include all the wrinkles, just the ones that suit the picture; if a young model is wearing a very bouffant hairstyle, lower it on your drawing if you feel it looks better; if the girl is very plump, thin her down; if a man has a decided paunch, don't portray it too faithfully.

Respect the truth, but don't hesitate to twist it a little in order to make it more presentable. Sometimes you need only slim the waist by half an inch to make it more attractive without distorting the likeness.

Deciding upon the pose

There you are, the model is in front of you, he is awaiting your instructions. Obviously it would be best to leave him as he is, if he's in a natural position. But the artist must intervene, not to make drastic changes in the model's habitual pose but to show it to the best advantage. Let's see what you can do.

Start by noting the position of the head in relation to the body, remembering Ingres' advice:

«*The body should not follow the movement of the head*».

In other words, see if you think he should turn his head a little; this produces a more graceful, less rigid pose. Look at these examples: in Fig. 89 we have a model doing an 'eyes front' —it's almost a military attitude. As you can see, this is a terribly monotonous, static pose and it is exactly what Ingres said you must not do. In Fig. 90 the model is still facing you but the body has been turned slightly to one side. That's better— don't you think so?

But several artists on several occasions have portrayed models 'facing front' like this —as if they wanted to appear deliberately primitive. An enormous number of such poses occur in modern painting: a

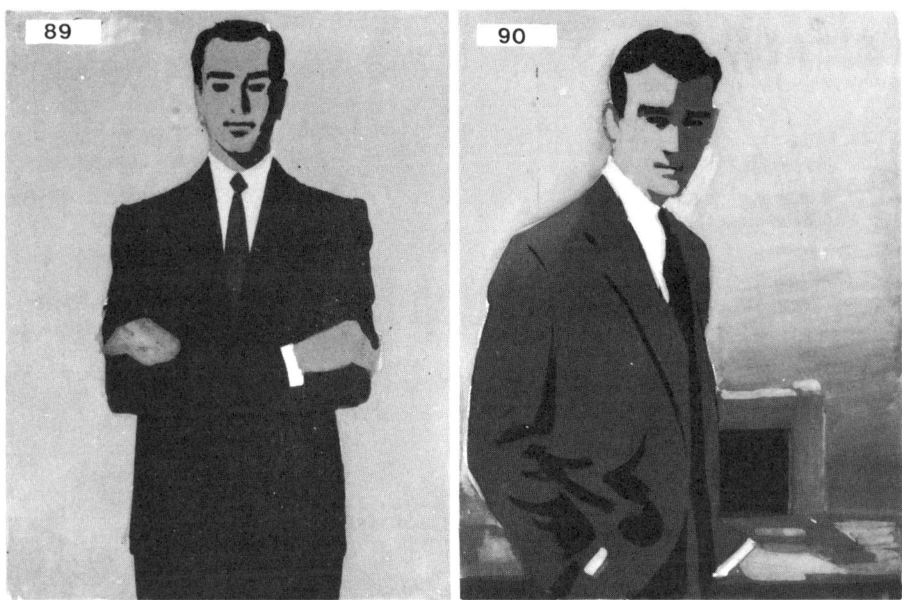

large proportion of Modigliani's portraits were painted in this position—we could perhaps describe them as a little academic.

Our advice still stands: for the time being follow Ingres' advice and turn the head in a different direction from the body.

If necessary, make the model do something with his hands

Some people are natural models; they know how to position their hands easily and gracefully. Others don't know what to do with their hands. So, besides chatting with the model, distracting him and making him feel at home, you may have to give him something to hold — a book, for example. You might give a woman a flower ; a man a cigarette ; a child a doll. But resort to this only when necessary. It is not a general rule.

Avoid foreshortening as far as possible

If the model is seated facing you, the thighs will be foreshortened; if seated sideways on a half-turned chair, the model can rest his arm on the chairback, which also produces foreshortening. Foreshortening can be difficult to draw accurately and attractively, so avoid it if possible.

For a half-length portrait, sit about six feet away from the model

For half-length portraits your chair should be about six feet from the model's. If you are drawing the head only, this distance can be reduced to 4½ feet. For a full-length portrait, it should be more, between 9 and 12 feet. Remember that full-length portraits are not particularly popular at the moment.

START YOUR EXAMINATIONS WITH SKETCHES

Bearing in mind what we have already said, try to find the best angle. Move round the model, experimenting with various frontal positions. Experiment, too, by changing the pose. Make at least five sketches, even if you think the first is satisfactory — it can always be improved on.

Make small sketches using a small pad or single sheets of quarto paper. Professionals take only six or eight minutes to do one of these. When you allow for the time spent changing the poses, changing your own position, chatting with the model, etc., you can reckon on an hour or an hour and a half on this preliminary stage. So we can lay down the law that:

The first sitting should be devoted solely to studying the pose (lighting, likeness, etc.) and making a number of preliminary sketches.

So you will not start on the final drawing until the second sitting.

A COMPOSITION PROBLEM

While you are trying to find the best pose for the model, you will in fact be solving a problem in composition. This is based on three things: *shapes, proportions and area.* The following examples should throw light on the subject and are illustrated on the opposite page (Figs. 91, 92 and 93).

Like everything else connected with the art of composition, these are not easy questions. Let us start with a simpler problem.

COMPOSITION IN A PORTRAIT OF THE HEAD ALONE

First of all we must decide whether it is best to draw the model full-face, in three-quarter view or in profile, remembering that full-face and three-quarter views are the most popular. We should also bear in mind that *the model's head should preferably be turned in a different direction from the body,* as Ingres recommended. Finally we have to decide whether the model should raise or lower his head a little, turn

91

A. — We have a white space, a sheet of paper cut to specific dimensions.

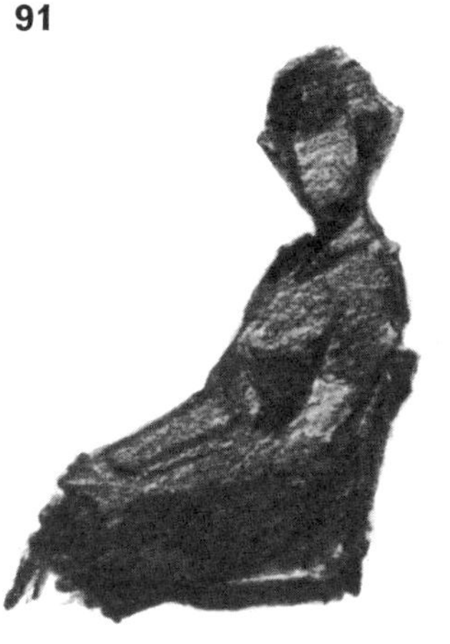

B. — We have a figure, the model, which when placed in a specific position, gives a tonal mass whose shape is also fixed.

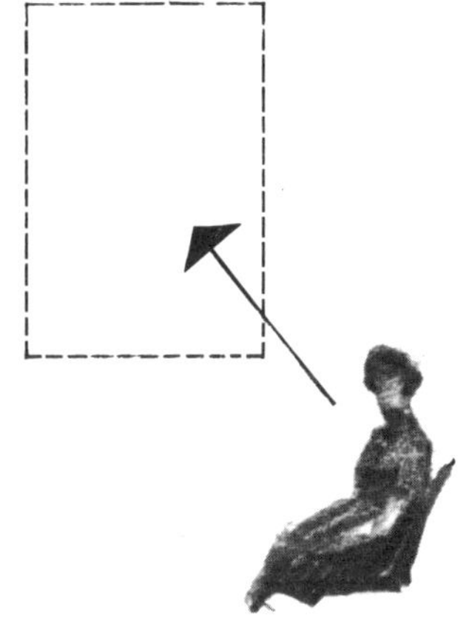

C. — And we must place that mass in the space available, producing a satisfactory composition and a captivating, charming and meaningful portrait.

92

Remembering what we have learnt, we should ask ourselves two questions:

1. — What shape should the tonal mass take to produce the desired effect? (Should it be longer, more angular, triangular, etc.?)

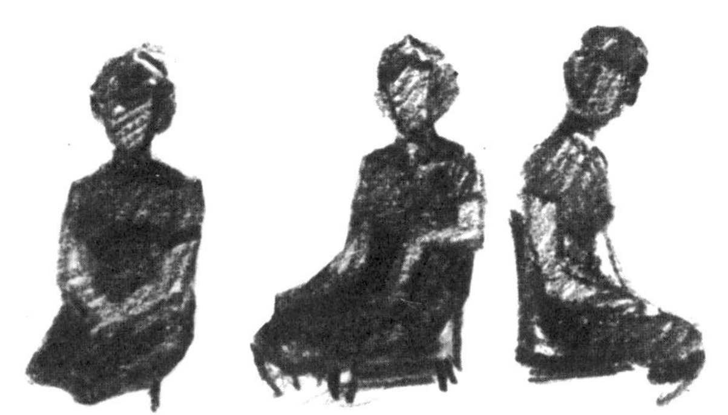

93

2. — Where exactly within the available space should the tonal mass be placed to produce the best effect? (In the centre, on the right, higher, lower, etc.?)

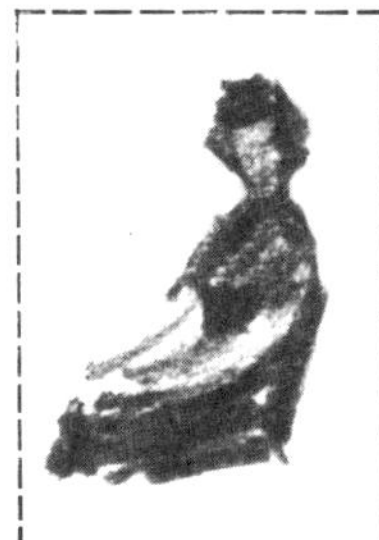

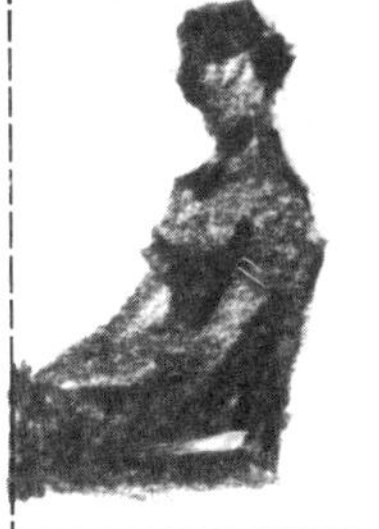

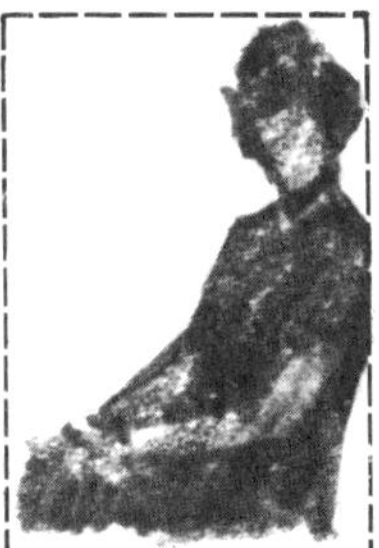

it or bend it forward to one side, etc. We can thus bring out the characteristic pose.

That is all we need bother about regarding the pose.

COMPOSITION IN A PORTRAIT OF HEAD ALONE

Turning now to the framework for the head, we need to decide on *its position in relation to the height of the frame.* Where shall we place it? In the centre, slightly above or below the centre? At this point I should explain the following rule for composition:

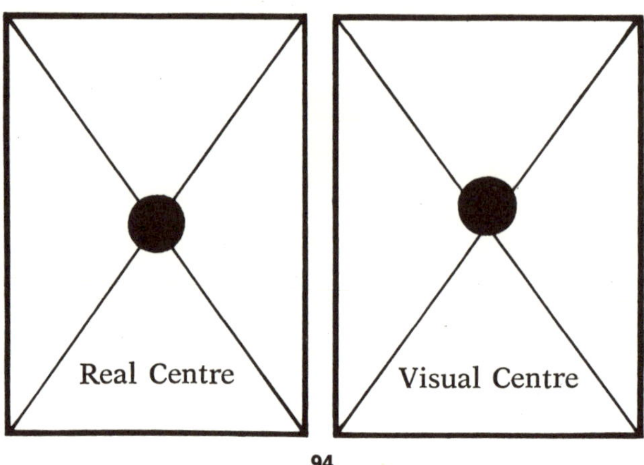

94

An optical illusion presents the visual centre of an area as being above the real, geometrical centre.

Very slightly higher, of course, but enough to show that if the tonal mass were placed in the geometrical centre, the centre of the drawing appears to have been shifted downwards. (In our case the tonal mass will be formed by the oval of the head, the neck and part of the shoulders and base of the neck).

Now we come *to position the tonal mass in relation to the width of the area.* There are three classic positions:

a) When the model is seen full-face, the head should be placed in the centre.

b) With a three-quarter view, the head should be slightly off-centre, leaving more space in front than behind the head (Fig. 95).

c) When seen in profile, the head sould appear to be off-centre and moved even further backwards than in *b* (Fig. 96).

Only *b* and *c* merit any study here: they tell us that more space should be left in front of the face. Ingres' advice is very specific on this point:

> «Leave more space in front of the face than behind —it should look as if it needs to breathe».

Remember these two basic rules on framing: the *visual centre* and *more space in front than behind.* They are always relevant.

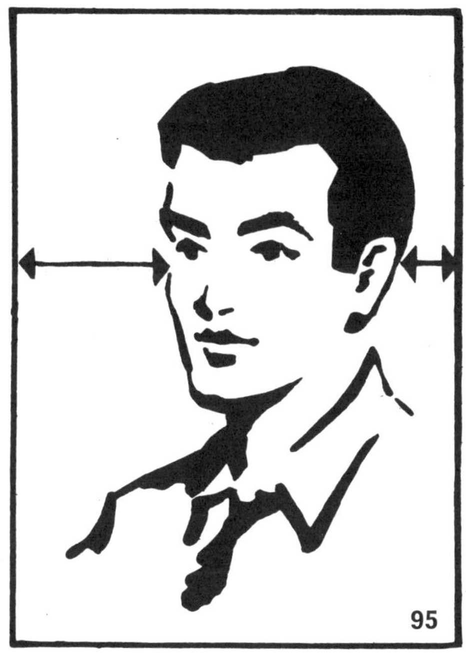

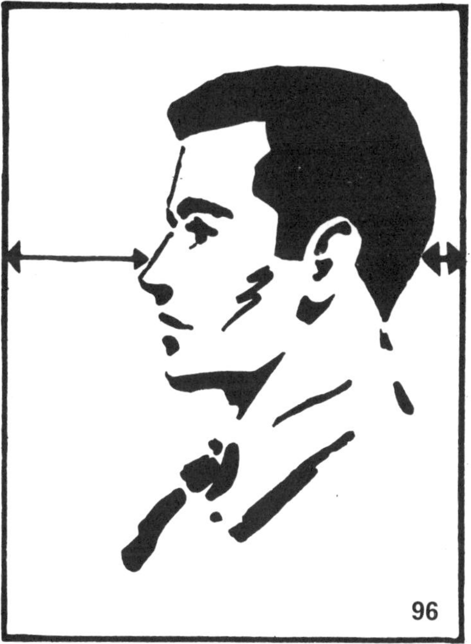

COMPOSITION IN A HALF-LENGTH PORTRAIT

Here, the question of the pose is much more complicated. When the model is seated, you have to decide whether the hands should be placed in the lap, on the left or the right thigh, with the arms bent; should the body be facing almost exactly towards the front, with the head at a slight angle; or should it be almost in profile with the head turned towards you? Should the model bend his torso slightly forwards away from the back of the chair or should he sit up straight against it? Ought he to lean back in the chair or loll with his head bent to the left or right? And so on...

There is such a variety of possible positions that it is hard to lay down rules. But I would suggest that you first of all decide upon the position of the head, this being the most vital factor, going on to experiment with different positions for the body. To give you an idea, look at the sketches made by Francisco Serra during a first sitting which was devoted to what we call the «examination of the model through sketching».

The illustrations which follow were produced by Francisco Serra as a preliminary study for one of his many portraits. They were done with charcoal on ordinary paper in a sketch book measuring 5 1/8" × 7 1/8" with two sketches on each page. Apart from the task of searching for the right pose, note the style of these rapid sketches. They were drawn almost without taking pencil from paper and with the intention of boxing up and proportioning the mass by picking out and drawing the body's basic shapes, i.e. seeing the head simply as an oval without any of its detail.

97

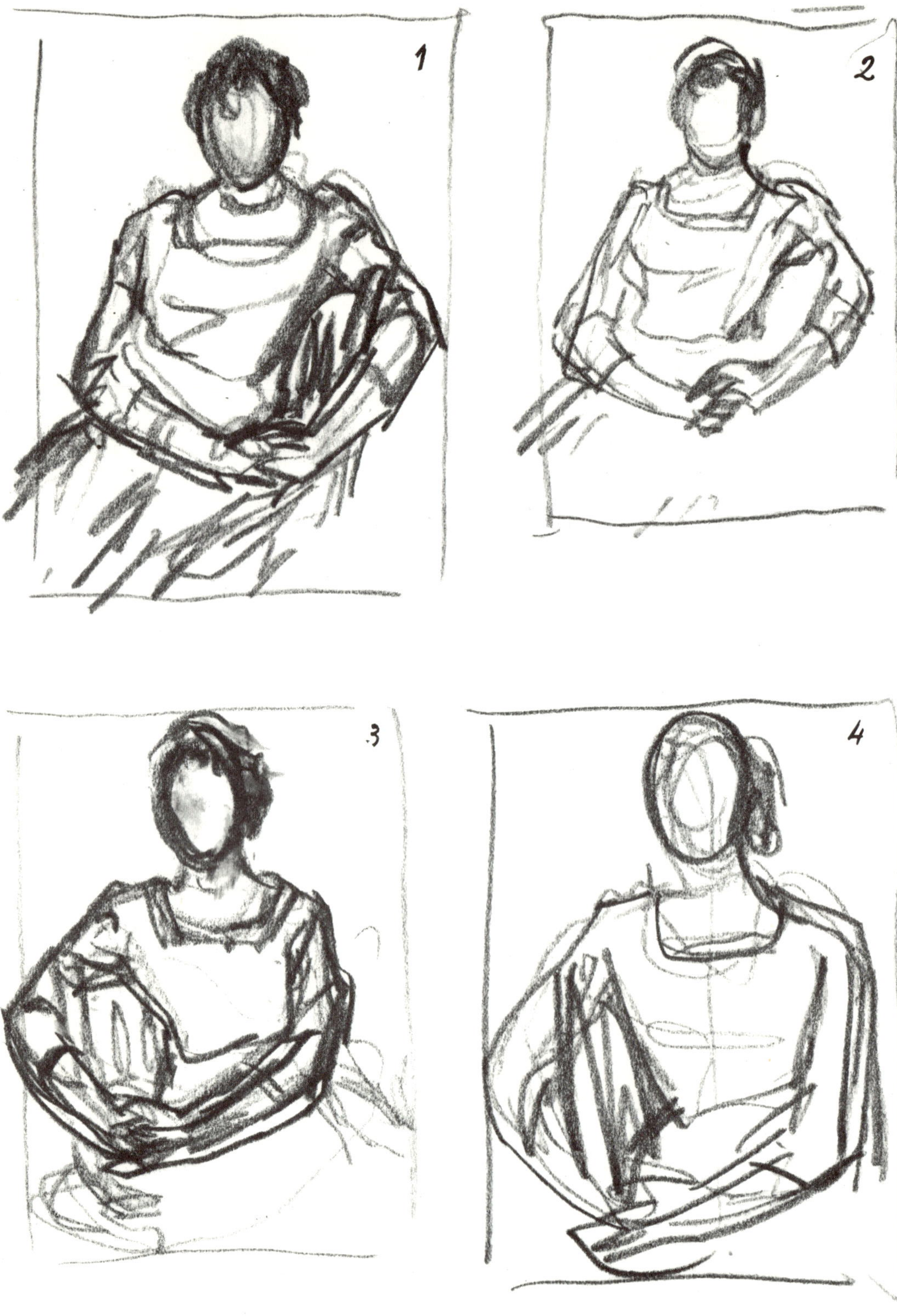

FIRST SKETCH: In this initial pose Serra was investigating whether the back of the chair should be to one side of the model, who would rest the left arm on it while folding her hands on the same side.

SECOND SKETCH: The same pose with a slight change: the model sits a little further back in the chair, a position which looks more comfortable and shows her figure more clearly.

THIRD SKETCH: Practically the same position, but the other way round; the whole body, arms and hands leaning and meeting on the right. The head keeps the same position as in the first sketch, facing forwards.

FOURTH SKETCH: The chairback is less obvious: the model had to get up and shift the chair so that it was seen more in profile with her right arm closer to the body. (Compare this sketch with No. 3 and notice the difference in the arc formed by the right arm).

FIFTH SKETCH: «No, it won't do: let's try something new. Could you bring your arm forward and fold your hands on your lap», we seem to hear Serra saying. The pose has been changed a great deal. Even the head is not facing forward as much as it was. The lines and contours of the body are definitely more graceful.

(«...yes», we can imagine him thinking, «but what about that strut showing behind the body... and that piece of skirt at the bottom... and the left shoulder which...»)

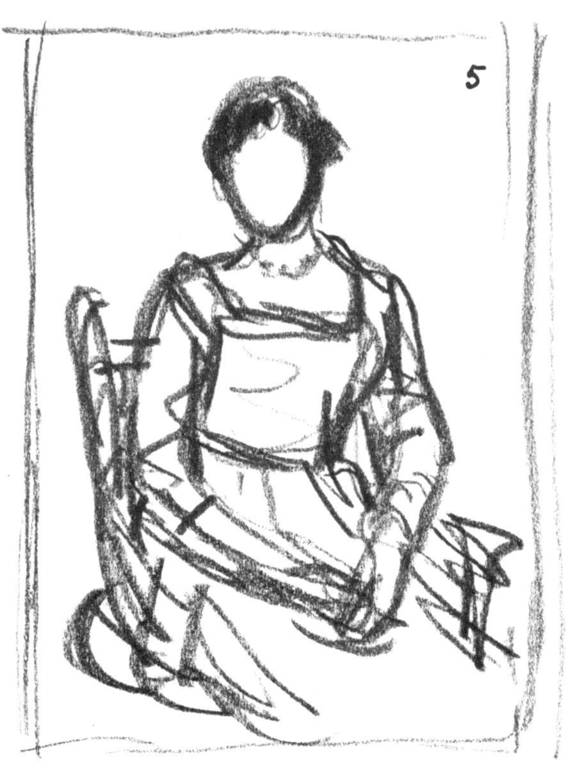

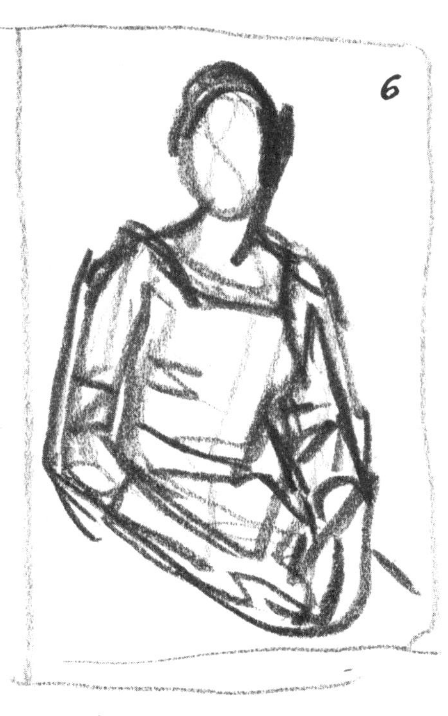

SIXTH SKETCH: Got it! Perfect! At first glance it may seem no different from No. 5, but look carefully: the left shoulder has been moved backwards, producing a nice curve in the neck, and the model's left arm is also further back than it was. This improves the unity and continuity of the shape and outline of the arms and body; (compare it with the previous sketch). The strut of the chair and the lower section of the skirt have been taken out. This is the best pose and it completes the preliminary stage.

It is interesting to watch the artist's initial preoccupation with the problem of framing the model. With a little smile Serra told me: «First I draw the cage; then I put the model in it, making sure she is comfortable and has just the right amount of space.»

Framing the model is a problem quite easily solved. We know to start with that more space must be left in front of the model than behind, as we have seen in Figs. 95 and 96 when discussing the head only. Here again, if the head-and-body mass is shown in three-quarter view, you must think about leaving more white area on the side the model is facing.

You also have to balance what we can call the «mass of the model» and the «mass of the background». Therefore you must view the background as another tonal mass competing with the mass formed by the model. Look at Fig. 98: A shows the model and the background; Letter B shows the mass formed by the model and Letter C the mass formed by the background. Letter D is an example of imbalance: the mass of the model is exceptionally small in comparison with the mass of the background. Fig. E shows the opposite: an enormous mass of the model quite out of proportion with the background mass.

There are few firm rules for producing this balance. It is a question of intuition and instinct, which can be developed by studying the composition of great paintings. This trains your feeling and awareness of good and bad composition. It can at first be based upon the following rule of thumb:

Good composition is achieved by the correct

balance of foreground and background.

Too much symmetricality between the various parts of the drawing, though suitable for certain themes —including portraits— is difficult to apply satisfactorily; the resulting works are usually monotonous, unoriginal and sometimes too solemn. As we have seen, excessive disparity produces an even more disastrous imbalance. It is best to strike a happy medium by deciding either to *make the mass of the model more important than the mass of the background, or vice versa.*

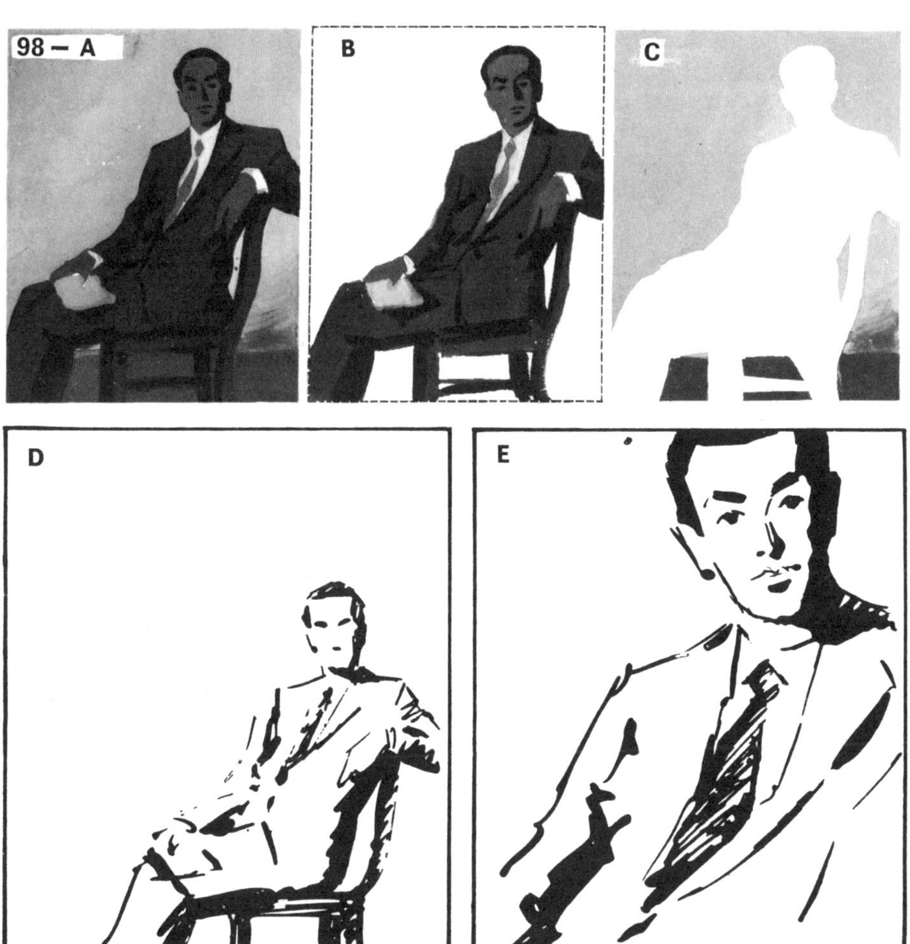

THE BACKGROUND

I have said several times that the most suitable background for a pencil portrait is plain white (or cream, blue, etc., depending on the colour of the paper). Let's hear it once more:

For pencil portraits, the most acceptable background is the white of the paper.

Occasionally an artist may draw in a shaded area, sometimes in order to create an exciting contrast and emphasise some highlit section of the model. But, I repeat, this is rare.

So, the first sitting is over. In the course of it the artist has made five or six sketches, each of which took him about ten minutes... so that in 90 minutes or so he will have produced one sketch which he will use as a pattern for the final portrait. Before letting the model go, the artist marks the position of the two chairs —the model's and his own— on the floor by chalk or pencil marks.

SIZE OF THE FRAME

The usual size for drawing a head or half-length portrait is half a standard Royal sheet of 19" × 24", i.e. 19" × 12".

For a full-length portrait double this size can be used. To sum up:

THE MOST COMMON SIZES FOR A PENCIL PORTRAIT

Head only or half-length:	19" × 12"
Full-length:	19" × 24"

(But, as I said earlier, full-length pencil portraits are not in fashion these days).

Although these are the most common sizes, there are some exceptions where the artist prefers to compose his work within a specially dimensioned frame. For paintings there are some standard, more strictly defined measurements, namely the «International sizes for stretchers and canvases». Many painters, however, have opted for diferent sizes. Look at the examples in Fig. 99: a portrait by Kaufmann, the American artist, who used an elongated canvas; a self-portrait by the French Impressionist painter, Gauguin, who used a square; and, finally, a portrait drawn by Degas in a non-standard frame.

SIZE OF THE DRAWING

By this I mean the size of the head and the body within the area forming the frame as described above.

All artists are in agreement on this point. For instance, nobody draws a life-size portrait when it is half- or full-length. They all scale down the actual dimensions and, in approximate terms, these are as follows:

THE SIZE OF THE HEAD IN A PENCIL PORTRAIT

Head only:	*4 3/4" to 6" high*
Half-length:	*4" to 4 3/4" high*
Full-length:	*2 3/4" to 3½" high*

Stick to these sizes and proportions when drawing a portrait from life.

START ON THE FINAL WORK

Start by boxing in the general outline, referring to the sketch selected earlier and fixing the position of the mass of the model within the definitive area or sheet of drawing paper.

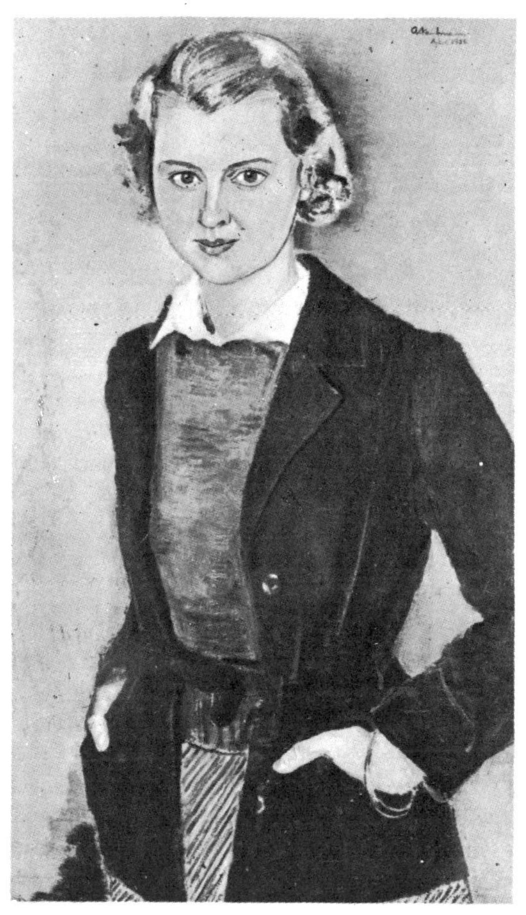

FIG. 99. — Left, portrait of a woman by Kaufmann, using an elongated frame; next to it, Fig. 100, a Gauguin self-portrait, using a square; below, Fig. 101, portrait by Degas on coloured paper, using charcoal and white chalk and an unusual format.

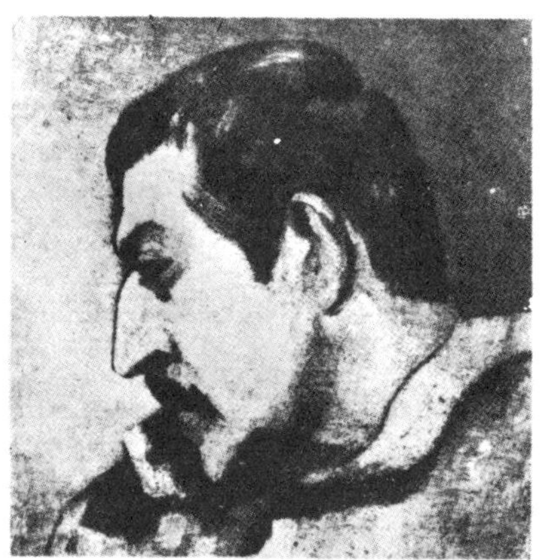

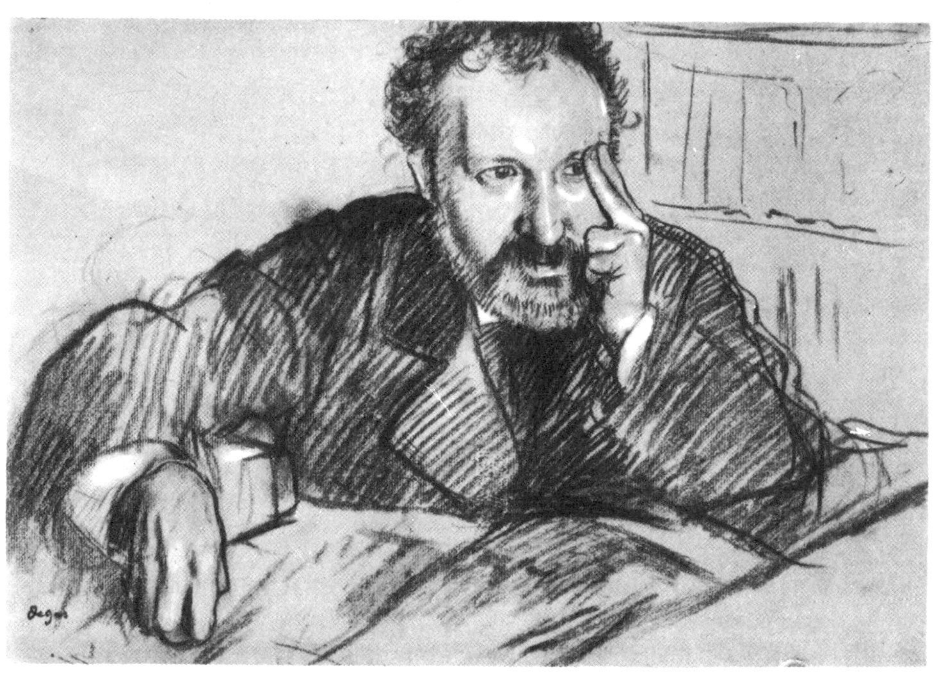

Box up the shadowed areas, appreciate the tones, study the contrasts...

Now is the time to organise, select and group, i.e. to arrange the forms and tones in an attempt to bring out the main «motif» of the picture.

In a portrait this main «motif» or *centre of interest* is the *head* and the face of the model. Remember this: everything else —body, hands, background— must take second place. The head must attract immediate attention and hold the observer's eyes. This is how to do it:

EMPHASISE THE HEAD BY TONE AND DEFINITION

To put it another way: *the head should be carefully finished and the rest just sketched in.*

I shan't explain how you are to achieve this. Have a look at the superb portraits which follow. They were drawn by Francisco Serra, Alfredo Opisso and Ramón Casas, and they are exactly right. Each provides a perfect example of everything we have been learning. In Serra's drawings, especially the portrait opposite of the sculptor L. Cairó, notice the precision and definition of the head, in contrast to the body, which is merely sketched in. Yet look at the extraordinary character of those lines: the patch of shadow in the tie, the simplicity of the hands. Don't you agree that it is an astonishing portrait? Study the drawing of the artist's wife on p. 83 and see how the head is brought out with all the interplay of light and shadow, while the clothes, although perfectly drawn and arranged, are barely sketched in. How clever of him to include the graceful, expressive form of the little dog, making a perfect composition of line and tone and an ideal balance between the masses. We can say the same of the portrait on page 65, which captures a genuinely original pose producing a highly effective arabesque.

Study the portrait of a woman by Alfredo Opisso (p. 85), with the position and treatment of the hands drawing our attention to and stressing the beauty of the face.

Now look at the magnificent charcoal portraits by Ramón Casas where, despite the different style, the artist is just as concerned to define and finish the head, in contrast to the shape of the body and clothes, which are merely indicated as in a preliminary sketch (pages 86 and 87).

Now that you have studied this fascinating subject, you probably want to start drawing a portrait from life straight away. Why not ask one of your family to pose for you? Don't worry, they will agree... even if only to make you happy. Because, as I have said before, there is nothing quite as satisfying as portraiture. When you see a portrait taking shape and coming alive under your hands and when the model himself says «Yes, that's me to the life» as if he was your assistant... then you will feel like laughing and shouting for joy and... no more from me. Try it out for yourself!

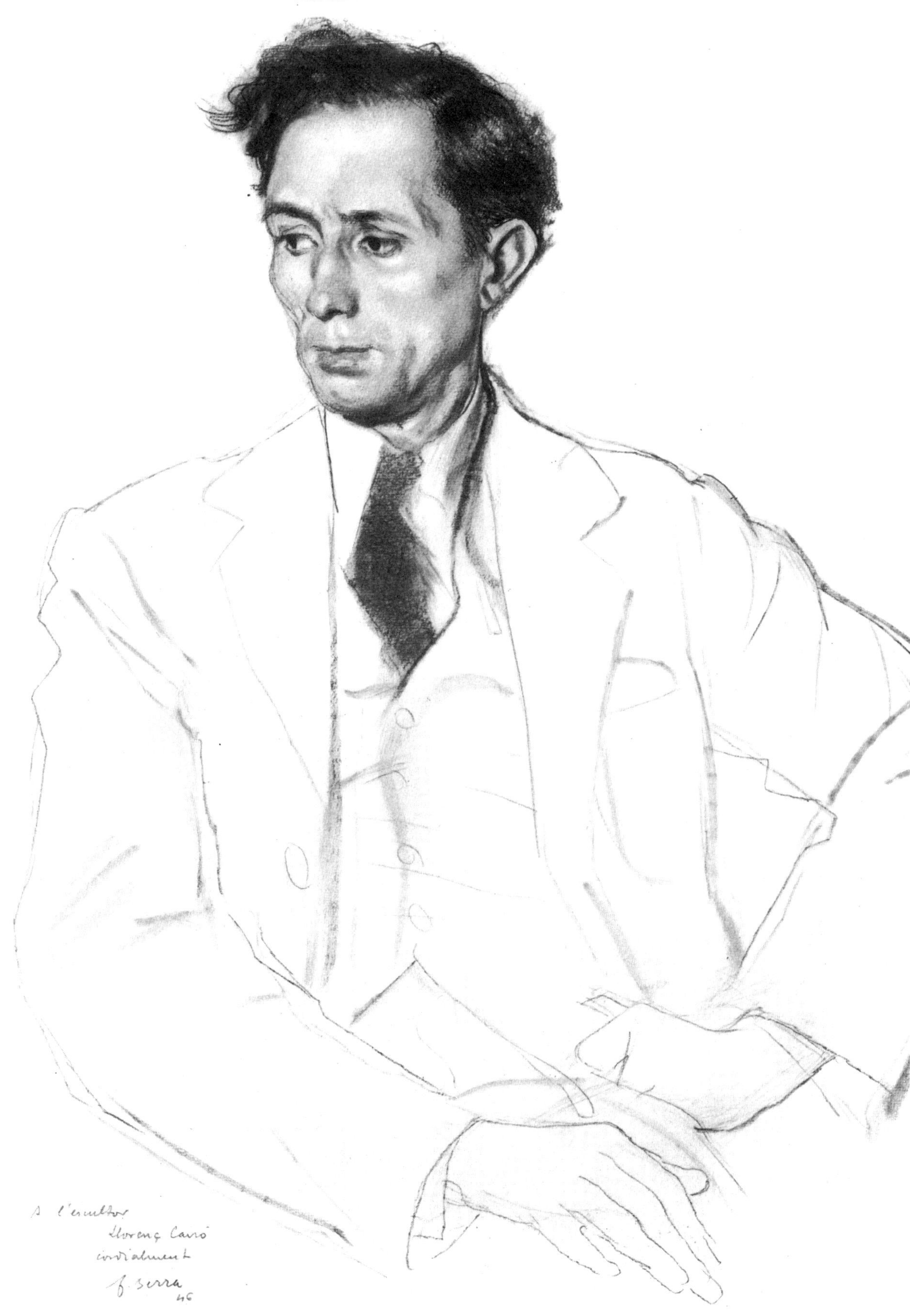

102. Francisco Serra, in this portrait of the sculptor L. Cairó, provides a superb example of how to emphasise the head by tone and definition.

Pencil Portrait

FRANCISCO SERRA'S METHOD

Paper:

«Marca Mayor» made in Spain.

Pencils:

«Koh-i-noor», HB and 2B. He also uses a piece of soft graphite, about as thick as a stick of pastel, to draw large shadowed areas (using it like a black crayon), blending and softening outlines cohich he then smooths and hatches with his finger when necessary.

Rubber:

«Milan» type.

Fixing liquid:

He does not normally fix his drawings since he feels that they should be framed straight away.

Drawing board:

An ordinary portfolio resting on the back of a chair in front of him.

Lighting:

Artificial. An ordinary 100 watt bulb hanging from the ceiling with a plain lamp shade and a pulley to raise or lower it.

Distance:

Distance from the model: 5' - 5'6".

First sitting:

Devoted to studying the pose and composition by drawing a series of small charcoal sketches in an ordinary drawing book.

Total sittings:

5 poses, each an hour or an hour and a half long.

Technique:

General framework in HB pencil. Shading and dark areas with 2B and the piece of graphite mentioned earlier. Blends tones with his fingers, alternating with pencil lines, without hatching.

103. Francisco Serra. — Pencil portrait.

Pencil Portrait

ALFREDO OPISSO'S METHOD

Paper:

«Canson», made in Spain.

Pencils:

«Faber, Dessin 301», standard No. 2. (He uses no other pencil since, he says, the softer ones smear easily and he does not often use them.)

Rubber:

«Milan» type.

Fixing liquid:

He never fixes his drawings.

Drawing board:

An ordinary portfolio resting on the back of a chair. He does not fix the paper to it but leaves it loose to be moved as he needs.

Lighting:

Artificial: two 60 watt bulbs, one for the model and one for himself.

Distance:

Distance from the model: 6 ft.

First sitting:

Devoted to studying the pose and composition, but drawing directly on to the final paper. Using the boxing-up process, he starts parts of the drawing two, or even three times, selecting the final drawing from these.

Total sittings:

4 poses of approximately one hour each.

Technique:

He obtains the gradations in tone simply with the No. 2 pencil and not with his fingers. He blends and darkens directly with the pencil. He obtains black areas by repeated strong strokes of the pencil.

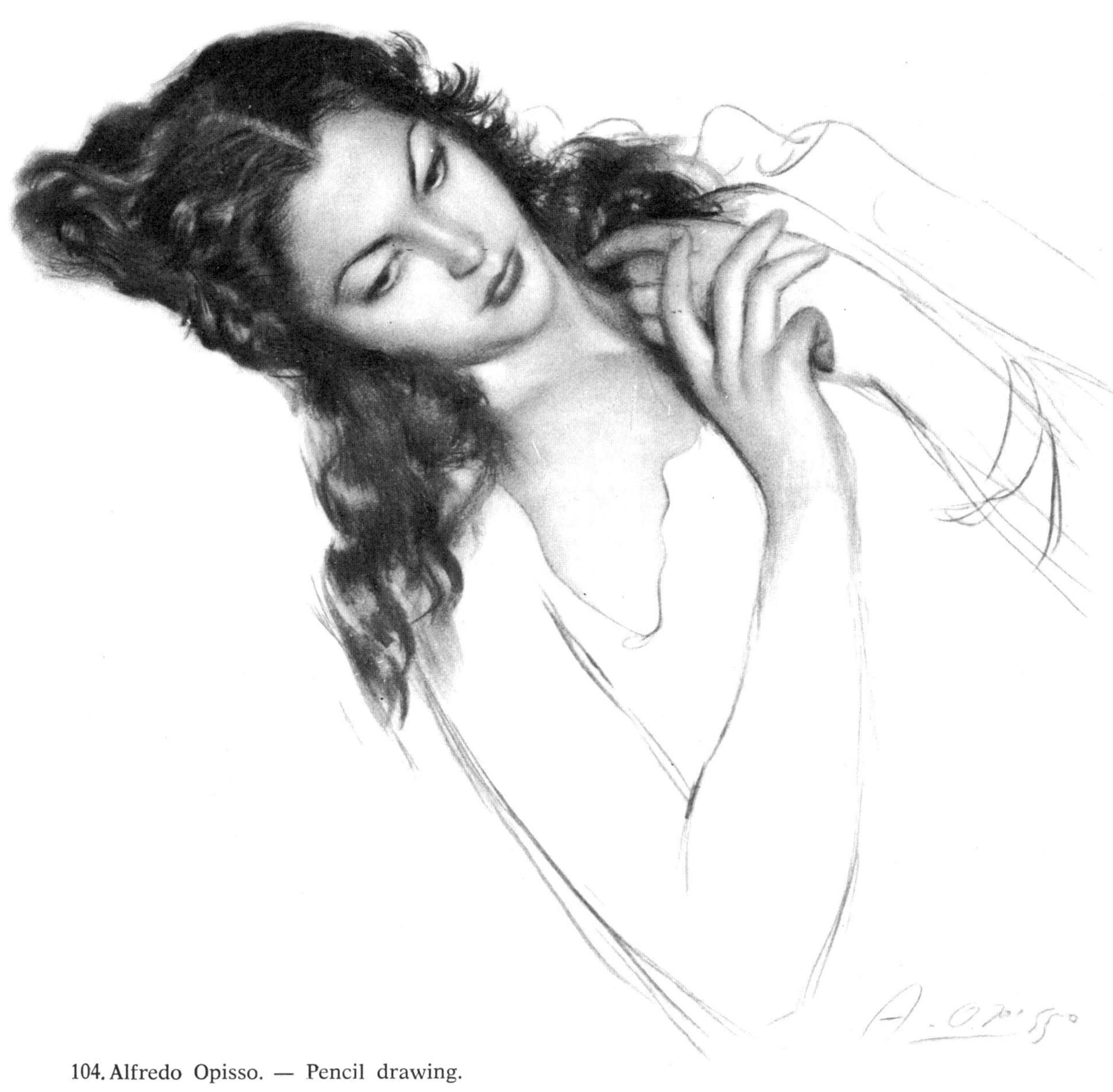

104. Alfredo Opisso. — Pencil drawing.

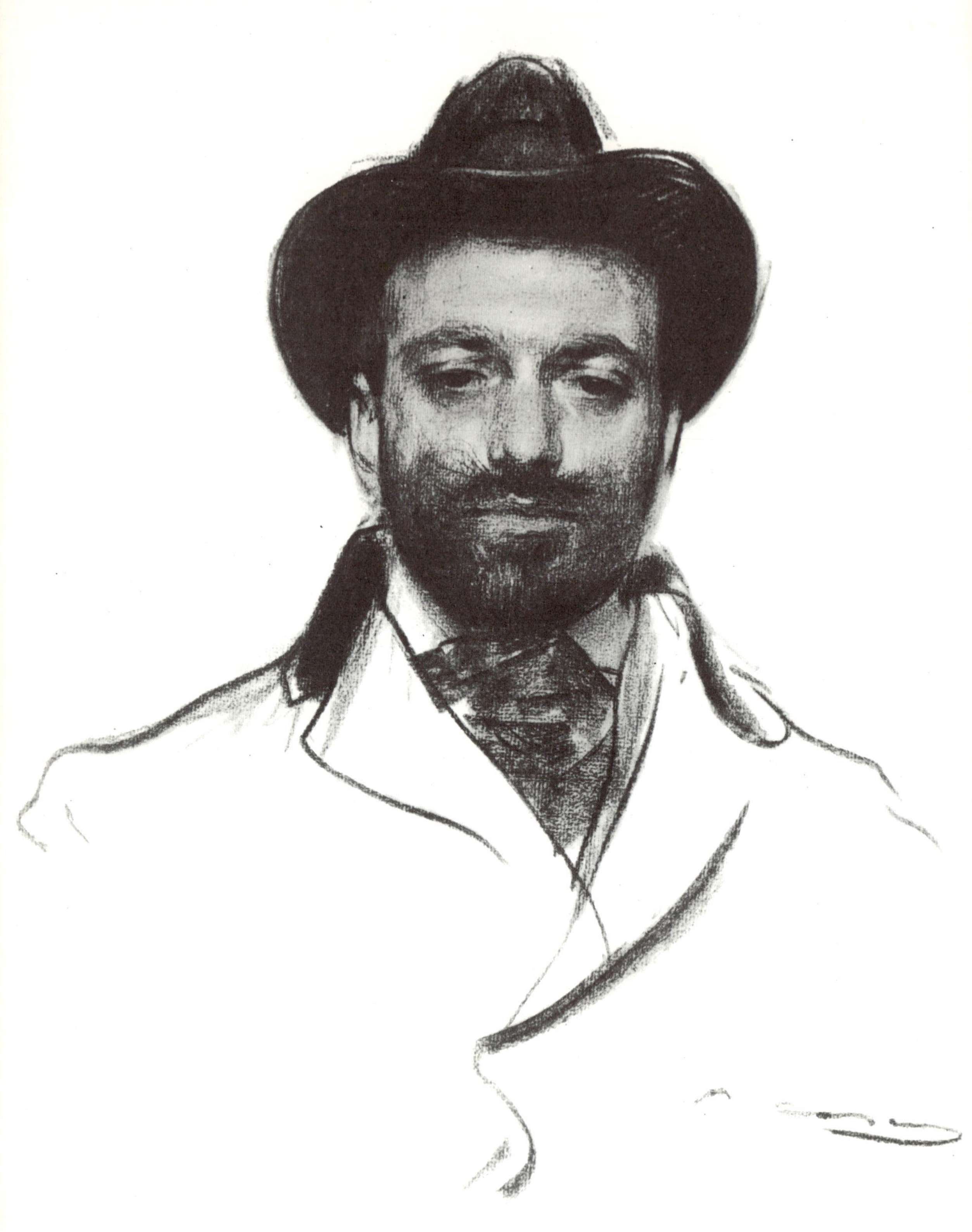

105. Ramón Casas. — Charcoal portrait of the painter José-María Sert.
(Museum of Modern Art, Barcelona)

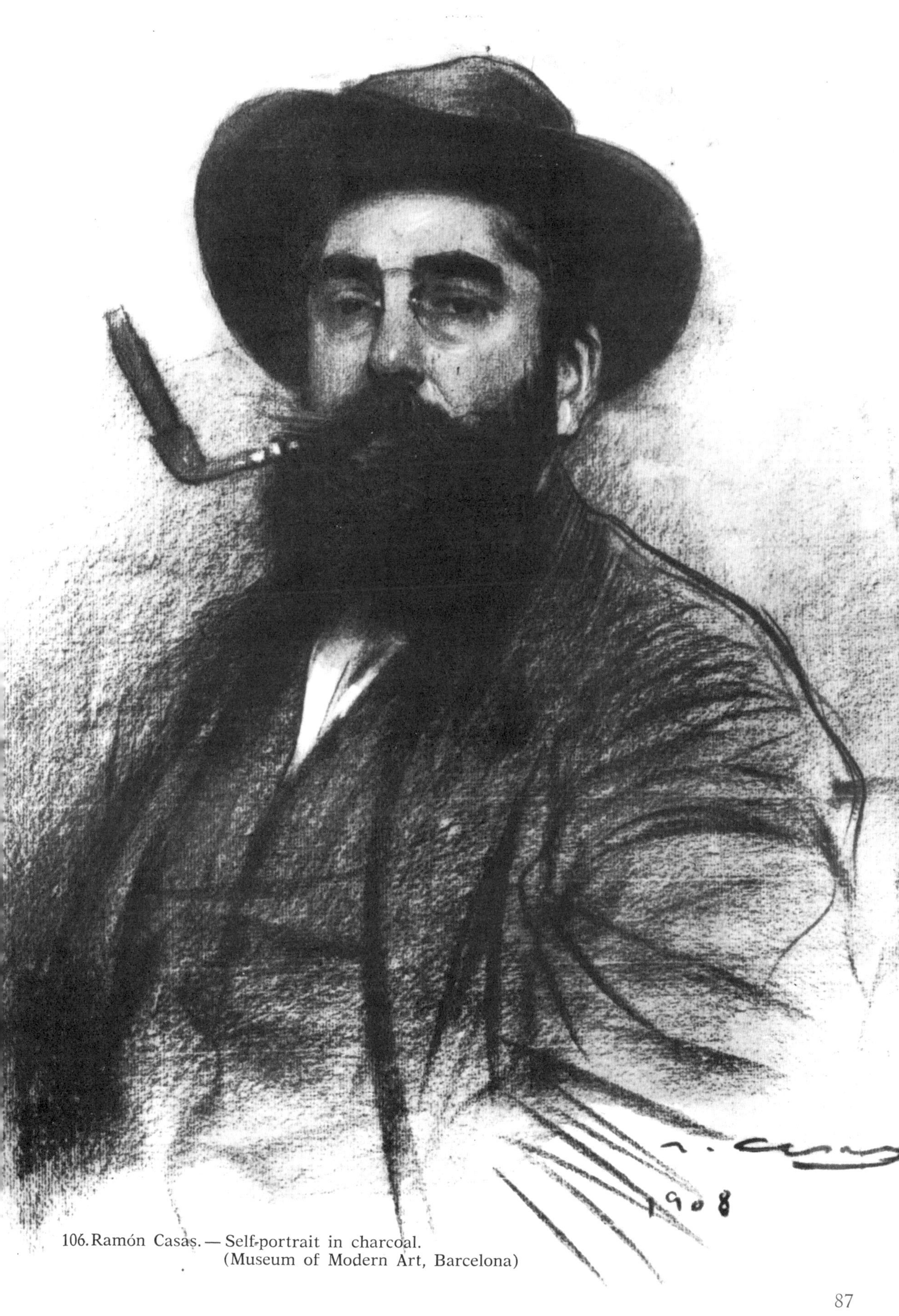

106. Ramón Casas. — Self-portrait in charcoal.
(Museum of Modern Art, Barcelona)